Green investing

A Guide to Making Money through Environment-Friendly Stocks

JACK ULDRICH

BUSINESS

Avon, Massachusetts

Published by
Adams Media, an F+W Publications Company
57 Littlefield Street, Avon, MA 02322
www.adamsmedia.com

ISBN-10: 1-59869-582-7
ISBN-13: 978-1-59869-582-3

Printed in Canada.

J I H G F E D C B A

Library of Congress Cataloging-in-Publication Data
is available from the publisher.

This publication is designed to provide accurate and authoritative information
with regard to the subject matter covered. It is sold with the understanding
that the publisher is not engaged in rendering legal, accounting, or other
professional advice. If legal advice or other expert assistance is required, the
services of a competent professional person should be sought.

—From a *Declaration of Principles* jointly adopted by a Committee of the
American Bar Association and a Committee of Publishers and Associations

Many of the designations used by manufacturers and sellers to distinguish
their product are claimed as trademarks. Where those designations appear in
this book and Adams Media was aware of a trademark claim, the designations
have been printed with initial capital letters.

This book is available at quantity discounts for bulk purchases.
For information, please call 1-800-289-0963.

Contents

Editor's Note

Different people use different terms to refer to investing in renewable energy companies. Some refer to it as green or greentech investing, while others label it cleantech investing—because the energy sources are nonpolluting, hence clean. For the purposes of this book, the various terms are interchangeable. They will be used to describe companies that employ innovative technologies to create new products, processes, and services that compete favorably with existing energy sources, technologies, and services in terms of price and performance, while simultaneously reducing mankind's impact on the environment.

The terms *cleantech* and *greentech* will primarily be used to describe companies seeking to generate energy from alternative energy sources, including solar power, wind, biofuels, and fuel cell technology. Some attention will also be devoted to companies that are developing more resource-efficient industrial processes that help conserve energy usage and/or reduce harmful environmental emissions, as well as those engaged in more speculative renewable energy sources, such as wave power and geothermal energy.

It is worth noting that as of 2007 there were estimated to be more than 900 companies which could legitimately be classified as cleantech companies. In the interest of both time and space, this book has focused on 90 of the most promising companies currently participating in the greentech arena. Obviously, the list is somewhat subjective, but every effort has been made to discern those companies most likely to have the biggest impact in the energy sector in the coming years.

Furthermore, because this is a book on investing, considerably more attention has been paid to publicly traded cleantech companies than to privately owned ones. The private companies that have been profiled were selected either because they may soon be publicly traded or because their technology was deemed sufficiently impressive that it was felt the company had the potential of "disrupting" an existing market (i.e., taking a significant amount of market share away from a particular source of energy) and thus might represent a significant economic threat to existing publicly traded energy companies.

"The field of greentech could be the largest economic opportunity of the twenty-first century." ·

—John Doerr, venture capitalist

Chapter One

Green Investing: A Long-Term Trend

In January of 2006, President George W. Bush in his State of the Union speech stood before the packed chambers of the United States Congress and told the American public, "We have a problem: We are addicted to oil."

Just nine months later, however, scientists from Chevron reported that they had discovered an oil field—Jack No. 2—in the Gulf of Mexico containing up to 15 billion barrels of oil. It was the largest such oil discovery in America in the past four decades and it instantly bolstered the country's strategic oil reserve supply by nearly 50 percent.

From this perspective, it might be plausible to conclude that America's oil "problem" had been temporarily resolved. But investors interested in appreciating the potential of green investing are encouraged to focus on the use of the word "addicted" in the president's speech because it gets to the heart of the opportunity that awaits the patient, long-term investor.

To understand why the choice of the word "addicted" is so apt, consider that all Chevron must do to recover the oil is first construct a massive multi-billion-dollar platform 175 miles off the shore of Louisiana—smack dab in the middle of an area which, as recent history has demonstrated, is subject to the occasional Category 5 hurricane—and then lower a good deal of expensive equipment down through 7,000 feet of corrosive salt water to the floor of the ocean. Upon reaching the bottom, the oil company must still then penetrate through four miles of rock. All of this for the privilege of tapping into a depleting source of energy that was formed 35 million years ago.

Of course, once this precious oil has been located, the battle is only half over because it must then be sucked back up to the top of the surface and transported either via a 175-mile pipeline or by being placed in gigantic tankers and brought to an expensive refining facility. There it will undergo further processing before being distributed all across the continent to waiting consumers, who will then burn the product in their automobile engines and allow its carbon byproducts to be released into the atmosphere.

From this perspective, the lengths America and much of the rest of the developed world go to get their oil are, in fact, illustrative of the classic symptoms of a die-hard addict. (The nasty side effects oil inflicts on its users—e.g., pollution, climate change, geopolitical conflict—also bring to mind the associated costs of a drug habit.)

We are not trapped in this self-destructive course. There are better, cheaper, easier, less pollutive, and, ultimately, more sustainable methods of deriving the energy the world needs to power its homes, businesses, and automobiles; and those solutions reside in the rapidly emerging field of clean energy. And in his speech, President Bush outlined the broad solution to the problem when he said "the best way to break this addiction is through technology."

A Long-Term Secular Trend

In 2007, two separate research organizations published comprehensive reports on cleantech. The first, by Cleantech Venture Network, noted that the amount of energy produced from alternative, renewable sources was expected to grow at near exponential rates for the next decade. Wind power, for instance, the report said, would triple from $17 billion today to $60 billion in 2016; biofuels would increase four times from $20 billion to $80 billion in the same period; solar would spike from $15 billion to $70 billion; and even fuel cell technology will experience an elevenfold increase from $1.4 billion to $16 billion within a decade's time.

The second firm, Lux Research, didn't publicly release its projections but did note that the growth of energy produced from alternative, renewable energy sources was a "long-term secular trend."

And the reason cleantech—and by extension green investing—is a long-term trend transcends the earlier story of America's addiction to oil. There are six factors driving the growth of clean, renewable energy.

The first is the rising cost of today's leading sources of energy. The discovery of the Oil Jack 2 aside, most experts now agree that oil is a dwindling natural resource and finding and delivering new oil will continue to get more costly. To the extent that the price does go up, alternative energies will become more attractive.

At the time of this writing, the price of a barrel of oil was around $100 and gas was hovering between $3.00 and $3.50 a gallon. This is significant not because it is an indication that the price will continue to go up, but rather because at this price it makes economic sense for companies to begin ˙investing in the development of renewable energies. Many alternative energy projects in the field of biofuels and fuel cell technology, for instance, make little to no financial sense when oil is below $50 a barrel but suddenly become practical above that price. Once the economic rationale is there, large investments are made in these energy sources. And once these up-front, fixed-cost investments have been made, there is little or no incentive to discontinue production even if the price of oil returns to more historical norms. In other words, cleantech is set on a course for which there is no reason to turn back.

The second cost-related trend facilitating the growth of cleantech is that environmental costs are now on the verge of being calculated when determining the total cost of a particular energy type. For example, in the past, the environmental costs of pumping billions of tons of carbon dioxide and nitrogen oxide into the environment had not been calculated when considering the true cost of using oil, coal, or natural gas.

With increased political and public attention now being placed on these environmental factors, it appears to be only a matter of time before such costs are captured and imposed upon the firms and companies most associated with creating those environment burdens. Any number of state, federal, and even international organizations are now developing rules and regulations that will either tax carbon emissions directly or cap the amount of pollutants that both energy companies and energy users can release into the environment. (The latter idea is often referred to as a "cap and trade" system. Under it, a government would place a limit—or a cap—on the amount of pollution that a company could emit; cleaner businesses would earn credits for producing fewer emissions and could then trade their credits to companies which have gone over their limits.)

To the extent that these environmental costs are soon captured in economic terms (for instance by imposing a tax on the amount of CO_2 a company emits), coal, natural gas, and oil will become even less attractive. Clean energy sources, which emit no such contaminants, will become more cost competitive.

The third driver of clean energy will be the overall increase in global demand for energy. Today, over 6 billion people populate the planet. By 2050, the number is expected to surge to 9 billion.

At the same time the countries with the largest populations—China and India—are adding to their population, they are also developing economically at an astronomical rate. The combination of economic and population pressure is placing an unprecedented strain on traditional energy sources. As the law of supply and demand adjusts to a newer, higher price equilibrium, it will work to the advantage of those clean energy sources that are readily abundant, such as solar, wind, and geothermal.

To put the issue in some perspective: between 2000 and 2006, China's oil consumption increased 7 percent annually, and it is expected to maintain this level of growth through 2017. What this means is that between 2007 and 2017, the country's total oil consumption will double. This kind of demand could leave Americans pining for the days when gas was "only" $3.50 a gallon.

Depending on what energy sources the developing world uses, the environmental costs could also skyrocket. In China alone it has been estimated that the country needs to build the equivalent of one new coal plant every week for the next decade just to meet its nearly insatiable demand for electricity. If true, the country, which in the summer of 2007 surpassed the United States as the world's largest contributor of carbon dioxide, could easily negate even the best efforts by the other world nations to limit and cut back on their carbon emissions.

To this end, the public's growing awareness of climate change is the fourth driver of cleantech as a long-term secular trend. From the fate of polar bears facing the melting of their habitat in the Arctic to coral reefs withering off the coast of Australia to the acclamation for Al Gore's movie *An Inconvenient Truth*, the signs that mankind is at least contributing to global climate change are now dismissed by only a few experts. (The years 1994 to 2006 have been among the twelve hottest years *ever* experienced on the planet.)

As a result, politicians, regulators, and even businesses are stepping up to the plate to address the issue. In 2006, California passed legislation requiring the state to reduce carbon dioxide emissions by 25 percent by 2020, and Minnesota recently mandated that 25 percent of its energy come from renewable energy within the same time frame.

Other state governments are actively considering similar legislation, and as a result, the business community has now seen the writing on the wall. Many companies, including such old energy stalwarts as Duke Energy, are now openly advocating for federal legislation on the theory that a single federal mandate beats a patchwork of different state mandates and regulations.

The fifth and sixth drivers of cleantech go hand in hand: an extraordinary amount of money is being invested in clean energy technologies by governments, large corporations, and venture capitalists, and this money is fueling the creation and development of a variety of very promising technologies.

First, the money. Following up on his 2006 State of the Union speech, President Bush in his address to the nation in 2007 announced that he was bolstering the federal government's cleantech investments by 22 percent, to almost $2 billion a year.

State governments including those in California, Pennsylvania, and Massachusetts are also investing hundreds of millions of dollars annually, and large corporations such as General Electric, IBM, Google, and Microsoft are investing billions more. Meanwhile the venture capital community has recently awakened to the opportunity and has reportedly raised its investments in the field to $2.9 billion. In total, Lux Research pegged all cleantech investment at $48 billion in 2006.

Of course, it is not the money itself that truly matters, but rather what that money is used for. Many of the most promising innovations will be documented in the pages ahead, but to get a sense of what the money has so far meant to the burgeoning renewable energy industry, it is helpful to consider that 4,000 new cleantech patents were filed in 2006. This number is expected to double again by the end of the decade. Now, not all of these patents matter, but even if just a few do they could, quite literally, change the world—and therein lies the real opportunity for cleantech and green investing.

While it is impossible to precisely predict how cleantech will affect the world's energy options in the years ahead, it would be foolhardy to think that society will still be constructing massive multi-billion-dollar platforms in the middle of oceans and drilling through 28,000 feet of salt water and rock to get the energy it needs to sustain itself.

It seems increasingly clear that much of the energy we need is already here—shining down on us in the form of sunlight, blowing in the wind, growing on farmland in the form of biomass, pulsating back and forth with the oceans' tides in the form of wave power, and maybe even hovering just below the surface of the earth in the form of geothermal energy.

If so, cleantech could, as John Doerr said, be the "largest economic opportunity of the twenty-first century."

Dangers

In my first investing book, *Investing in Nanotechnology,* I began the book by stating that if you were investing in the field of nanotechnology because you thought it offered a quick and easy road to riches, then the book was not for you. I feel obligated to provide the same caveat with this book. If you are considering investing in cleantech, greentech, or alternative energy—whatever name you wish to call it—in the hopes of retiring a millionaire by the end of this decade, then this book is not for you. Recall that John Doerr said that greentech could be the largest economic opportunity of the century, not the year or even the decade.

This is not to say, however, that cleantech won't be a huge and growing field much sooner than in a decade's time. It will be. Rather, my point is to temper "irrational exuberance." More important, I want to remind investors that just because a field will be big does not mean that every company or even a majority of the companies playing in that space will be successful. They won't.

Benjamin Graham in his classic best-selling book *The Intelligent Investor,* which has been praised by no less an authority on investing than the legendary Warren Buffet as being "the best book on investing ever written," began with a variation on this warning.

He wrote: "It has long been the prevalent view that the art of successful investing lies first in the choice of those industries that are most likely to grow in the future and then in identifying the most promising companies in those industries." Graham went on to add in the first edition of his book (written in 1949), that "[s]uch an investor may for example be a buyer of air-transport stocks because he believes their future is even more brilliant than the trend the market already reflects" and "because it was fairly easy to forecast that the volume of air traffic would grow spectacularly over the years."

Not surprisingly, history has borne out Mr. Graham's first investing "moral": "Obvious prospects for physical growth in a business do not translate into obvious profits for investors." For example, it is now commonly accepted that the cumulative earnings of the airline industry over its entire history have been negative. That is, since the Wright Brothers first achieved flight in December of 1903, the airline industry has been a net *loser* of money. A number of issues contributed to this shameful state of the industry—technological problems, intense competition and overcapacity, a host of managerial, regulatory, and labor-related problems, and, more recently, problems associated with the tragic events of 9/11. However singular the example, it serves as a reminder that any industry can grow rapidly and even become a vital part of the economy but still lose money.

Now, I don't believe cleantech will be a net loser of money, but with this little historical lesson in mind, my first piece of advice is that investors should limit the portion of their portfolio invested in cleantech to a maximum of between 5 and 10 percent.

Secondly, the historical analogy to the airline industry is appropriate for a few other reasons. For starters, as in the early aviation industry, any number of clean energy technologies are likely to encounter unexpected problems. For instance, some other techniques, such as efficiently converting cellulosic feedstocks into ethanol, may take longer than expected to achieve, or some technologies, such as safe, affordable hydrogen fuel cells or reliable wave power machines, may ultimately prove impractical. It is possible, too, that most clean energies will work exactly as promised, but one specific technology proves to be "first among equals" and renders other clean energy technologies obsolete, impractical, or uncompetitive.

A third warning is that change rarely happens as fast as people expect. Almost every industry, regardless of its unique characteristics, goes through cycles of hype and troughs of despair. The most recent analogy, of course, is with the Internet. In 1999, most Internet companies could do no wrong. By 2001, most of the funding had dried up and even solid companies with legitimate business models were struggling.

It is entirely possible that the same will happen with cleantech. According to a 2007 report by Lux Research, there are currently more than 930 cleantech companies. It is difficult to imagine how the industry can do anything but go through a serious consolidation as the less successful small companies go bankrupt and many moderately successful ones merge or are acquired by others.

For all of these reasons, it will be essential that investors continue to do due diligence on the companies profiled in this book. Chapter Two will provide an overview of how to do this. It will also be important to diversify one's portfolio with a mix of small and large companies. Chapter Three will focus exclusively on the largest cleantech companies, but small companies will be covered in Chapters Four through Six, which look at biofuels, solar power, and wind power, respectively. Chapter Seven will introduce the reader to a number of companies working in some early-stage fields—such as wave power, geothermal, fuel cell, and clean coal technologies—that are currently small but could experience extraordinary growth in the years ahead. Chapter Eight will cover energy conservation. Finally, Chapter Nine will conclude with a list of resources as well as a sample portfolio that the reader will want to consult when putting together his or her green investing portfolio.

"Fortune favors the prepared mind."

—Louis Pasteur

Chapter Two

Due Diligence: Do Your Homework

In the opening chapter, I discussed some of the dangers of investing in a new, albeit promising, field such as cleantech. Among other associated dangers of placing one's money in an emerging field is that many of the companies in the field do not have a track record by which to evaluate them using traditional valuation methodologies. For instance, many cleantech companies are still in the pre-revenue stage, meaning that they are not yet generating any revenue. Others either have untested technologies or are investing a good deal of money developing the technologies. The latter often results in companies having very rapid cash-burn rates. The implication for early investors is that if a company burns through all of its money before it has a workable technology, it could go bankrupt, or it will have to go back to investors to raise additional money, which will have the impact of diluting one's original investment.

Other dangers that lurk in the cleantech waters include the considerable competition in the field. This competition takes three forms. First, every renewable energy company is competing against existing energy sources—oil and gas, coal, and nuclear— that have a number of advantages. For starters, the old guard still has the advantage over renewable energy sources in terms of costs (provided one does not attempt to calculate the environmental costs). They are also large and well established. As such, they have deep pockets and strong political connections and are unlikely to readily cede market share to cleantech companies.

The second form of competition is that which will take place among other renewable energy sources. For example, corn-based ethanol will not only compete against gasoline, it will also go head-to-head with biodiesel and butanol. The same may be true of solar cell technology competing directly with fuel cell technology, and wind power vying with wave power for the attention of electric utilities.

Lastly, there is the direct competition within each field. Not all ethanol companies are equal. Corn-based ethanol companies will be competing with cellulosic-based ethanol producers, and silicon-based solar cell companies will be going head-to-head with thin-film solar cell companies, and both must then face the prospect of competition from firms working on solar mirrors and solar concentration technology.

What this means is that investors will need to do their due diligence before investing in individual companies. What follows is a list of practical steps that should be followed prior to investing in the field.

Strip the "Cleantech" Label

The first step any individual investor needs to do when conducting due diligence is to strip the term "cleantech" off whatever the company is doing and investigate it from a standard business perspective. The general rule of thumb is to invest in good business opportunities, not in broad categories such as renewable energy. There are simply too many companies using the term too loosely for investors to take any company's claims at face value.

Next, many problems can be avoided by finding answers to the following questions:

1. Does the company talk about specific market applications for its technology or just large markets? Beware of any company that throws around big numbers and claims its products will capture a sizable share of the multi-billion-dollar energy industry. It will also be helpful to understand how its product will be marketed and sold and to know whether the company has access to foreign markets.

2. How will the company's product evolve over time? If it is an ethanol company, is the company looking at producing ethanol from feedstocks other than corn? If it is a silicon solar company, does it have a plan or is it investing in thin-film solar technology?

3. Is the company able to subcategorize the specific market it intends to enter? Companies that claim to be a broad-based cleantech company with products and technologies appealing to a wide range of markets need to be treated with suspicion.

4. Does the company talk about product development within a reasonable time frame? Better yet, has it actually produced

a real product? Companies that are only in the concept or development stage are probably still too young for the average individual investor to invest his money in.

5. How does the company's technology stack up in terms of price and performance with others in the field? For instance, in the solar cell field a company that is producing silicon-based solar cells should have a long-term contract with a silicon producer to ensure a reliable supply of silicon. If a company doesn't have such a contract, it could be vulnerable to fluctuations in the price of silicon.

6. And finally, does the company have strategic partners or actual customers? Many of the markets that cleantech-enabled solutions will find a home in—biofuels, wind, solar, etc.—are large and complex. As such, they are difficult for small companies to successfully enter alone. Having a strategic partner is often the best, easiest, and fastest way to commercial success.

In addition to these questions there are other factors that individual investors should also take into consideration. These factors can be broadly thought of as people, markets, technology, and finances. The questions to consider are:

► Does the company have a reputable and experienced management team?

► Can the company's product or technology be mass-produced quickly, cheaply, and reliably?

► Does the company possess technical leadership in its field and does it have proprietary intellectual property?

► Does the company have the financial resources to accomplish its strategic goals?

It All Starts with People

Obviously, it is not wise to focus on just one of these four factors. They have to be viewed together as part of a whole picture. However, when beginning one's due diligence, a lot of time can be saved by researching the quality of the management team. The quality of a company's management has the highest correlation to whether the venture succeeds or fails. An innovative or "cool" technology is not enough to guarantee success. An experienced CEO is often necessary to drive the right technology solution to the largest market. Furthermore, because it is rare that any technology—or business—ever evolves according to plan, an executive team that has actual experience growing a business is a definite advantage. Often, these executives have learned from past mistakes and will have developed the capacity to adapt to rapidly changing environments.

A number of cleantech companies are started by scientists. Investors should not be lulled into believing that their scientific credentials alone provide them with the skills to run a company. These scientists are often brilliant and understand their technology better than anyone else. They are not, however, managers or executives. Scientists don't always understand the marketplace. Moreover, they aren't trained to take risks—scientists are taught to be methodical. The latter trait is a necessity in science but it can be deadly in business—especially in a business environment that is changing as rapidly and radically as renewable energy. Good executives know when to act and they often need to do so with less than perfect information.

Potential investors are also encouraged to review the scientific advisory board the company has assembled. Does it have the depth and breadth of experience to really direct the company?

And are the advisors really part of the management team or are they "paper-only" members. The more engaged these advisors are in the company, the better.

It's the Product, Stupid

Back in the 1930s it was demonstrated that a new keyboard, called the Dvorak system, was superior to today's common QWERTY keyboard. It allowed skilled typists to type an average of 165 words per minute versus 131 words on the QWERTY system. It did this by rearranging the letters so that there was less left hand use, fewer row-to-row hops, and none of those bothersome pinky stretches.

As history has vividly demonstrated, the Dvorak system, in spite of its superiority, didn't win in the marketplace. The reason is that it required people to learn an entirely new system of typing. And while it would undoubtedly have been more efficient for those doing a lot of typing, for most users the benefits of changing to the new technology did not justify the up-front investment in time to learn a new system, which would yield only a modest increase in efficiency.

The moral of this little story is: Just because a new technology is better does not guarantee that it will win in the marketplace. This also serves as a cautionary tale about the difficulty of assessing whether a market will embrace a new technology. Normally, if you told a consumer or a company that a product would yield a 20 percent increase in efficiency, they'd jump at it. Such is not always the case, however, if it requires the consumer to change behavior.

This is relevant for a variety of renewable energy sources. Some biofuels, for example, will require producers to find new methods of transporting the fuel because they are incompatible with existing distribution systems. Additional ethanol, biodiesel, or, in the longer term, hydrogen may also require retailers to install new fueling stations and many might balk at the high cost of installing the system, especially if the payback isn't immediate. The net effect could be that biofuels are not accepted into the commercial marketplace as quickly as its proponents predict.

To help determine whether a technology has "legs," investors should be able to answer the following questions: Does the product solve a real problem for its customers? For instance, does it save its users time or money, or provide them with a benefit or freedom they didn't previously enjoy? If the product meets a real need, then investors have something worth considering. If not, investors should consider leaving it for others to fund.

Is It an Idea, a Demo, or a Real Product?

The third step in considering an investment is to discern where in the development stage the company's product is. For example, is it in the concept, preproduction, or postproduction stage? If things haven't matured to the point where the product is past the concept and an actual sample or prototype has been developed, it is too early for most investors.

If a company's technology or product is past the concept stage, the next question investors need to consider is whether the company has demonstrated "scalability and reliability." Can its biofuel, solar cell, or wind turbine be manufactured in the quantities and sizes necessary to attract the attention of major customers? And can those products be made in a manner consistent enough to guarantee quality and performance? A number of companies have recently begun producing wind turbines, which have a host of promising properties including a high strength-to-weight ratio. As a result, their deployment is being explored by a number of large electrical utility companies. But until all of the bugs can be worked out and until customers can be guaranteed that the turbines are reliable and low maintenance, the future of some of these turbines will remain a question mark.

The most promising sign that a cleantech company is on the verge of creating a viable business—at least in the short term—is that its technology does not require manufacturers to change any of their existing equipment or processes. As was stated earlier, it is human nature to resist change and large companies are no different. Those companies that create technologies that don't require manufacturers to change are going to have a leg up, certainly in the short term. Examples of this are companies looking to make coal-burning plants cleaner today. Whether a company is using nanocatalysts to neutralize nitrogen oxide or using algae to capture carbon dioxide, if a coal-burning plant doesn't have to change any of its existing technology or processes, the company has a better chance of succeeding in the commercial marketplace.

Regardless of where the product is in the development stage, investors should determine whether the company has done its homework in regard to how it's going to approach the marketplace. Does the company demonstrate pricing logic? Has it determined why a customer would be willing to pay a specific price for its product? Has it targeted specific customers? Better yet, does it already have customers?

One Is the Loneliest Number

Because many cleantech start-ups are small, they will need assistance in getting their product to market. For this they will often need partners. Therefore, at a minimum, investors should know whether a company has successfully entered into arrangements with large corporate partners who will either use their technology or help develop technology to produce their products. For instance, Synthetic Genomics—a promising biofuels start-up—announced that BP was investing in the company. In addition to providing the company with a substantial amount of working capital, the partnership also offers Synthetic Genomics the potential to distribute and market its product in the commercial marketplace much faster than if it was a standalone company.

Another company that has established a useful partnership is Metabolix, which in mid-2007 announced that it would be partnering with Archer Daniels Midland (ADM) to produce and commercialize a biodegradable plastic. The partnership doesn't guarantee Metabolix's success, but by being able to take advantage of ADM's expertise, brand recognition, and key relationships in the consumer products industry, the company is better positioned to succeed.

Beware of Competing Technologies . . . and Lawyers

As the two earlier sections on people and markets demonstrate, investors cannot rely on superior technology alone to drive a company's stock upward. Still, technology is obviously important, and assessing a company's technology—and the intellectual property behind it—is among the most difficult and time-consuming tasks for an investor.

Certain clean technologies are complex and require a broad base of scientific knowledge. Specifically, some require a deep understanding of many different fields of science—biology, physics, chemistry, material sciences, and the computational sciences. Assessing the relative merits of these technologies is beyond the skill set of the average investor (and even most professional investment advisors).

How, then, does one go about it? First, one should find out which other technologies (and companies) are out there trying to address the same problem. For instance, Chapter Four mentions numerous companies seeking to effectively and efficiently produce ethanol from feedstocks other than corn, Chapter Five documents a handful of companies developing flexible, thin-film solar cells, and Chapter Six lists a host of companies manufacturing next-generation wind turbines. The best advice is to be aware of these competitors and then let the companies themselves explain why their technology is superior.

The one thing investors should not do is be overly impressed with the number of patents a company has. All patents do is exclude others from copying the invention. They do not stop someone from creating a different way to address or solve the same problem. One company can hold 250 worthless patents, while another can possess just one very valuable patent.

The trick, of course, lies in distinguishing a worthless patent from a valuable one. Recognizing that this skill is also beyond the capability of most people, at least in a field like cleantech, investors are encouraged to look at the scientific credentials of the founders of the company and its scientific advisory board. This is by no means a perfect measure, but to the extent that the individuals associated with the company have published papers in credible, peer-reviewed scientific journals or have established relationships with credible academic institutions, government laboratories, or corporations, it is a useful gauge.

For instance, the fact that Craig Venter, one of the scientists credited with sequencing the human genome, is the founder of Synthetic Genomics doesn't necessarily guarantee that his patents or technology relating to the creation of "designer bacteria" (which can cheaply and easily produce ethanol or hydrogen) will succeed, but it does improve the odds that the company's technology is on solid ground.

Investors will also want to consider whether the smaller cleantech companies are partnering with large corporate companies or have received investments from leading venture capital firms. This is significant because both have scientists and trained technical advisors with the requisite skills to more thoroughly evaluate a company's technology and intellectual property. All things being equal, if established companies and venture capital firms have assessed the technology and decided to invest in the company, it is a positive sign. For example, Vinod Khosla, one of America's leading venture capitalists, has invested in Mascoma Corporation, Iogen, and Cilion (among others). Again, this doesn't guarantee that any of these companies will win in the commercial marketplace, but it does imply that each company's technology is sufficiently promising to warrant an investment.

The tactic essentially amounts to letting others do your due diligence for you, but unless you have the technical skills and the time to investigate a company yourself, it is often the best that can be done. Chapter Nine lists a few of the venture capital firms that have developed some expertise in cleantech, and in the company profiles in the following chapters every attempt has been made to list which venture capital firms and large companies have invested in a given company or are partnering with the company. The information can be considered supporting evidence of the viability of a company's technology.

Such measures are imperfect, but they pale in comparison to the difficulty of assessing intellectual property. It is almost a given that any successful technology will draw some type of legal challenge and that that challenge will come only after time, money, and a great deal of effort has already been invested in getting the technology to the marketplace.

The best way to assess a company's position in this regard is to determine whether the company itself has done its own due diligence on its intellectual property. Questions to ask are:

► Has the company thoroughly analyzed its own IP claims?
► Has the company analyzed the patents held by its competitors?
► Does the company have international patent protection?
► Does the company have systems in place to protect its IP?

And if a company has licensed its intellectual property to others, investors should understand:

► The terms and conditions of the license—whether it is an exclusive, nonexclusive, or field-of-use exclusive license.
► The duration of the license.
► How the patent holder is compensated—in cash, equity, royalties, or some combination thereof.
► If there is a challenge, who is responsible for paying the legal costs? As with the assessment of the technology itself, assessing legal issues is best left to the experts—in this case, the lawyers. Because hiring such expertise is beyond the financial means of the average investor, we

are again left with the situation of relying on the legal experts of the company, partnering companies, or the venture capitalists.

Often, the best an investor can do is ask the questions. If the answers are not satisfactory or if there are too many unanswered questions and it appears a legal challenge could either delay or entirely stop the successful introduction of the technology, it is best to hold off on an investment until such issues are resolved.

Many companies, even private companies, often have a staff person devoted to investor relations. Investors are encouraged to contact these individuals and seek answers to the above questions.

Follow the Money

In real estate, realtors are fond of saying that the three most important things are location, location, and location. Some in the investment field have parroted this line and said that the three most important things for any new business are money, money, and money.

Money is obviously an important component of any business and no business can succeed without it. And for established businesses, profits are an absolute necessity over the long run. But for start-ups the situation is a little more complex.

It is unwise to give too much attention to how much money a new private start-up has raised. For one thing, too much money can be a bad thing in the sense that it can result in an undisciplined business atmosphere where company executives and employees don't feel a need to squeeze out every efficiency. It may also allow company executives in the short- to mid-run to cover over—and hide from investors—some fundamental problems.

When conducting due diligence on start-ups, there are a few key factors one should consider. The first is to remember that it is unwise to fund a research project. More simply put, investors should only consider investing in those companies that have moved beyond the idea stage and are actually manufacturing—or are close to manufacturing—products. And, as was said earlier, the manufacturing process should be mature enough that products can be built on a reliable, cost-effective, and scalable basis.

A perfect example of this is Magenn Power, an early-development-stage company that is seeking to develop a high-altitude wind power system. At this stage, it is an intriguing idea, but the company has no working prototype and very little cash on hand. Obviously, such a venture is far too risky for the prudent individual investor.

The second thing to look for is something called the "skin game." Do the company founders have their own money invested in the company? Even more important perhaps is whether they have convinced their family and friends to invest in their company. If the answer is yes to both questions, it is a positive sign. It speaks to the founders' confidence in the company, and it provides them a stronger incentive to succeed—no one likes to let down their family or friends.

The third factor to look for is government money. Investors should not fund research- or concept-stage projects but governments should—and often do. Therefore, investors are encouraged to consider whether a company has received grants from the Department of Energy or NASA. Many of the biofuel and solar companies listed in Chapters Four and Five, for example, are receiving some government funding. In fact, a few have received very sizable grants. For instance, POET Energy is slated to receive up to $80 million from the Department of Energy to fund the development of a process to produce cellulosic ethanol; Konarka Technologies, a private start-up, has received multimillion-dollar grants from various U.S. military departments to employ nanoscale materials in the development of flexible plastic solar cells.

The point here is not to imply that the government has an impressive track record at picking winning technologies (it doesn't). Rather, it is to highlight that the government is, in essence, helping to underwrite some companies' research and development—and it is doing it in a way that doesn't dilute investor equity. (The government doesn't ask for a stake in the company—only the right to use the technology if and when it is developed). Investors should, however, be cautious of companies that are either entirely reliant on government grants or that, after years of government funding, are still unable to attract any corporate attention.

Investors should also consider the amount of venture capital funding a company has received. This is a double-edged sword. On the positive side of the ledger is the fact that these venture capital firms have done their own due diligence and found enough promise in the company to warrant a follow-on investment.

Not all venture capital firms are equal, however. As was demonstrated in the dot-com era, a herdlike mentality can often be found among venture capital firms. At the present time, only a handful of firms have acquired the expertise to adequately do the due diligence in the field of cleantech.

Venture capital firms are important for two reasons in addition to the financial resources they bring to the table. First, they often come to the table with fat Rolodexes and can help their portfolio companies find the appropriate executive management team. For instance, in early 2007, Vinod Khosla's firm was able to help convince a veteran ethanol CEO to leave his established company and help grow a new cellulosic ethanol company. Second, the good venture capital firms have existing relationships with major corporations and can use those relationships to play the role of matchmaker.

The downside is that for assuming so much risk, venture capital firms often demand a sizable share of the company's equity. This is a dilemma for both the company founders and individual investors. Obviously, venture capital firms deserve to be rewarded for the risk they assume. The question is how much. There is no simple, easy rule to follow. The stage at which the firm jumps in, the amount of money it invests, and the type of scientific and professional assistance it brings to the table all need to be considered.

In the final analysis, venture capital is usually a positive thing. Most start-ups fail—even those that venture capitalists invest in. Venture capital firms help fund the development of the idea, professionalize the management, and assist the company in getting its product to the right market in a time frame that allows the company the best chance of succeeding.

Buyer Beware

The harsh reality of the marketplace is that most high-technology companies fail. Cleantech is not going to be any different, and many of the companies profiled in this book will fail for the same reasons most companies do: poor management, inferior technology, and undercapitalization. By doing due diligence, however, the individual investor can reduce their risk. (Let me repeat that last point: risk can be reduced but it cannot be eliminated!)

Doing due diligence is not an easy task, but here are the ten most important questions an investor should have answered before investing in any company:

1. Is the company's management team experienced?
2. Does the company's product meet a real-world need?
3. Is the product ready for the marketplace and can it be produced consistently and reliably?
4. Does the company have strategic partners?
5. Does the company's founder have a strong scientific and technical background?
6. Is the company's board of scientific advisors actively engaged in the company?
7. Is the company's intellectual property patented or has it secured the necessary licensing agreements on favorable terms (e.g. exclusivity, duration)?
8. Do the company's founders have their own money—and that of their family and friends—invested in the company?
9. Has the company received any government grants to help fund its research and development?
10. Has the company received venture capital from a firm with established expertise in the area of cleantech?

The stock market rewards a greater return on an investment to those investors who see things—and possibilities—that others don't. This creates the incentive to conduct due diligence. As Louis Pasteur once said, "Fortune favors the prepared mind."

"For business, tackling climate change is both a necessity and a huge opportunity. . . . We have to step up to the challenge."

—James Smith, Chairman, Shell UK

Chapter Three

The Big Dogs: The *Fortune* 500 Companies

In many ways, *Fortune* 500 companies might seem to be the antithesis of cleantech, either because of their involvement in producing and profiting from traditional energy sources or because they themselves are such large consumers of fossil fuels. In spite of such realities, a handful of large companies do warrant consideration as "green" investments. (Perhaps you might want to think of them as "light green" investments.)

For starters, it is worth repeating that of the $48 billion invested in cleantech worldwide in 2006, nearly half of that total came from *Fortune* 500 companies. On this basis alone, these companies merit attention.

The investment side of the equation represents just half the story. In many ways the push into cleantech could be said to have started in 2000 when British Petroleum changed its name to BP and kicked off a large public relations campaign claiming that "BP" stood for "*Beyond* Petroleum." The campaign was designed to signal that the company was serious about developing alternatives to oil and gasoline.

Many opponents have accused the company of "greenwashing"—or hiding behind a slick advertising campaign designed to make them look environmentally conscious while going about business as usual. There is, of course, some truth to this accusation, because BP still makes the majority of its money from oil. But what most people don't know is that the change in philosophy was driven largely by practicalities: by cutting its own carbon dioxide emissions to 1990 levels, the company saved over $650 million. In short, BP awoke to the realization that there was money to be made by being green.

The company is still criticized for greenwashing, but in early 2007 the company further matched its rhetoric by investing $500 million in the Center for Energy Innovation at the University of California at Berkeley for the purpose of developing the new biofuels for the future.

In 2002, General Electric also aggressively moved into clean energy when it acquired Enron's wind turbine manufacturing assets for $400 million. Upon seeing the success of that business, which delivered revenues of $6 billion in 2006, the company's CEO, Jeff Immelt, announced GE's "Ecomagination" campaign and signaled the massive conglomerate's intention to move more aggressively into cleantech by increasing its commitment to renewable energy research and development from $700 million in 2005 to $1.5 billion by 2010. Perhaps more impressive is that GE now expects to generate $10 billion in revenues from green technologies within the same period. Again, it is further proof that the cleantech revolution is being driven less by a new environmental ethos and more by old-fashioned economic factors.

In just the past year, the progress among *Fortune* 500 companies has been even more startling, and it is clear that a sea change is under way in American businesses. The ball started rolling in January of 2007 when TXU, a large Texas-based utility, was acquired in a private equity deal for $32 billion. As part of the deal, investors from Goldman Sachs negotiated that the company wouldn't proceed with eight of eleven planned coal-fired power plants, in part because the utility company recognized that massive wind farms could generate a portion of the lost output.

The following month, Wal-Mart announced it was seeking to upgrade dozens of its stores to solar energy. As a result, scores of other retailers, including Kohl's and Target, also unveiled big solar initiatives in 2007. The same month, ADM and DuPont indicated that they would be moving aggressively into the large-scale production of biodiesel in the expectation that biofuel would be increasingly competitive with regular diesel due to new regulations the Environmental Protection Agency (EPA) began enforcing in late 2006.

In March, IBM announced its "Big Green Innovations," a campaign designed to save clients billions of dollars through the more intelligent application of energy-efficient programs. And in April, the Electric Power Research Institute—an organization that serves a great many coal-powered electrical utility plants—stated that it would begin including the value of carbon credits when comparing the cost of building new coal-burning plants. The move was a tacit acknowledgement that coal's true price isn't limited to the cost of producing the energy; its adverse impact on the environment and the health problems associated with coal-induced smog should also be calculated.

Step by step, it is clear that the business community has awakened to the new environmental ethic. The biggest signal of this change occurred when Alcoa, Duke Energy, Pacific Gas

& Electric, and nine other energy companies—all old stalwarts of the existing energy establishment—formed the United States Climate Action Partnership (USCAP) and announced for the first time that they were willing to entertain some regulation of carbon dioxide emissions. Such a proclamation would have been unthinkable even a few years ago.

Equally important, many of these initiatives are now being backed with sizable investments by some of the world's largest financial institutions. For instance, Morgan Stanley has announced that it intends to invest $3 billion to establish a system to trade carbon credits over the next five years, and JPMorgan has created an index to measure various companies' exposure to carbon regulations by weighting their bonds to the degree that they will either be positively or negatively impacted by such regulations. Both suggest that big business's new tune on environmental regulation is more than just rhetoric. Most companies are now taking active steps to prepare for the eventual reality of having to account for their emissions.

On a different front, Goldman Sachs is investing $1.5 billion in cleantech and has substantial investments in leading wind, ethanol, and solar companies; Bank of America has announced an even larger $20 billion commitment to cleantech.

It is plausible that many of these companies are getting involved in renewable energy because of the public's growing concern about climate change or because they fear the inevitability of restrictive government regulations (and would prefer to have a seat at the table when that legislation is being drafted). However, it is clear that they are also doing it because they realize there is big money to be made from being more environmentally responsible.

In the profiles that follow, readers will learn that BP is getting very serious about developing new methods to create clean, sustainable biofuels; GE intends to grow both its clean coal and nuclear power businesses; Siemens is focused on becoming a world leader in the development of wind power; and ADM is placing large bets on both ethanol and biodiesel.

Even big oil and chemical companies are taking some impressive actions. ConocoPhillips, for example, is increasing its investment in alternative energy research to $150 million annually—a figure that represents about 38 percent of its research and development budget. Dow Chemical is investing heavily in biodiesel production, Chevron is the world leader in geothermal energy, and even Exxon has taken a baby step down the cleantech path by acknowledging that the "climate is getting warmer."

For potential investors in any cleantech field, all of this is important because these corporations have the deep pockets to engage in the required research and development to create the green technologies of the future. Equally important, even if these companies' overall commitment to the cleantech cause is not as sincere as smaller cleantech start-ups' commitment, they still have the size, marketing, manufacturing, distribution, and sales staff to get their technology out into the commercial marketplace in a manner that will allow them to be very competitive.

For reason of size alone, then, investors interested in green investing need to be aware of what the following *Fortune* 500 companies are doing. They will be formidable players in almost every cleantech sector.

BP	COMPANY	BP Plc
	SYMBOL	BP
	TRADING MARKET	NYSE
	ADDRESS	1 St. James's Square London, SW1Y 4PD, United Kingdom
	PHONE	44-20-7496-4000
	CEO	Dr. Tony Hayward
	WEB	*www.bp.com*

DESCRIPTION   Formerly known as British Petroleum, BP is one of the largest oil and gas companies in the world and operates three different segments: Exploration and Production; Refining and Marketing; and Gas, Power, and Renewables. In 2005, the company formed BP Alternative Energy; more recently, it committed to investing $2 billion over the next three years to grow operations in solar energy, biofuels, and wind power. At the present time, alternative energy represents 8 percent of its total business.

REASONS TO BE BULLISH

► BP Solar is one of the largest and most profitable solar companies in the world. It currently controls 10 percent of the global solar market—a market that is expected to grow 30 percent annually for the next few years. In 2006, the company signed a deal with REC Corporation to supply it with silicon for the next six years.

► BP has a strong research and development team and is pursuing a joint development program with the California Institute of Technology to develop more efficient solar cells.

► In 2007, BP committed $500 million to the University of California and the University of Illinois to create an institute dedicated to exploring such issues as carbon dioxide sequestration and the creation of new biofuels from both microbes and crops. BP also made a sizable investment in Synthetic Genomics—a leader in creating "designer bacteria"—to pursue this goal.

continued

► BP received a $19.1 million grant from the U.S. Department of Energy to study how to make traditional silicon solar cells thinner and more productive.

► In 2007, the company acquired Orion Energy's 1,300 MW of wind power and also announced the creation of five new wind development projects in the United States with a total capacity of 550 MW of power. BP also has a long-term strategic alliance with Clipper Windpower to supply turbines capable of an additional 2,250 MW of power.

► The company is partnering with Powerspan to develop carbon dioxide capture technology. If successful the partnership could be very beneficial if the government imposes limits on CO2 emissions.

► In 2006, BP announced a joint project with DuPont to develop new technology for making butanol. If successful, butanol is likely to have a significant advantage over ethanol in the commercial marketplace. Not only does it have a higher net energy density, but it can be shipped in existing pipelines.

► BP management bought back a lot of its stock in 2006 and has always provided shareholders with a healthy annual dividend. In 2007, it was 3.8 percent.

REASONS TO BE BEARISH

► In 2007, the company's former CEO, John Browne, was forced to resign after a series of deadly and costly accidents severely damaged the BP reputation and depressed its 2006 earnings.

► Much of the company's oil operations are located in regions of the world, such as Angola and Russia, that are not politically stable. Global tensions in any area could hurt BP earnings.

WHAT TO WATCH FOR   BP is pursuing a number of cleantech developments that bear watching. Foremost among these are its solar improvement program with Caltech; its plans to develop a capacity of 2,000 MW of wind power in the United States; its biobutanol project with DuPont; and its plans to create the world's first commercial project designed to turn natural gas into hydrogen by stripping out carbon dioxide and pumping it into depleted oil reservoirs.

continued

CONCLUSION   Bullish. As one of the five major oil and gas companies, BP is not a "pure play" cleantech investment player because it still derives an overwhelming majority of its revenues from fossil fuels. Nevertheless, the total size of its alternative energy business (although it makes up only eight percent of the company's earnings) is substantial enough to make BP one of the largest renewable energy companies in the world. Over the coming years, this aspect of its business will likely grow into an ever-larger portion of BP's overall business. For investors looking for a larger company with the resources and capital necessary to exploit the growing interest in cleantech, BP represents a solid investment. Even compared with its peers in the oil and gas business, it sports a very reasonable price-to-earnings ratio of 11.

CVX	COMPANY	Chevron Corp.
	SYMBOL	CVX
	TRADING MARKET	NYSE
	ADDRESS	6001 Bollinger Canyon Road San Ramon, CA 94583
	PHONE	925-842-1000
	CEO	Dave O'Reilly
	WEB	*www.chevron.com*

DESCRIPTION   Chevron is the second largest U.S. oil company and operates across all segments of the oil and gas industry—exploration, production, refining, and marketing—and in 195 countries around the world. It also has modest stakes in a variety of renewable energies, including geothermal, biofuels, solar cells, and hydrogen/fuel-cell-related technologies.

REASONS TO BE BULLISH
► High oil prices are expected to keep Chevron profitable for the foreseeable future, but the company is beginning to make some sizable investments in renewable energy.
► In 2004, Chevron invested in Konarka Technologies, one of the more promising solar-related start-ups, and, together with Energy Conversion Devices, owns a 50 percent stake in Cobasys, a leader in developing high-powered nickel metal hydride batteries.
► Chevron is the largest producer of geothermal energy in the world, with facilities in Indonesia and the Philippines.
► Since 2006, the company has invested over $50 million in a variety of biofuel research initiatives (including cellulosic ethanol) at some of America's leading universities.
► In 2007, Chevron opened a 20-million-gallon biodiesel facility in Texas. The company is operating it with expectations that the facility could be producing 470 million gallons annually by 2010. If this expectation materializes, Chevron will be one of the largest biodiesel producers in the world.
► Chevron has begun to install both bioethanol E85 fuel demonstration facilities and hydrogen demonstration projects in California.

continued

► In 2007, the company received regulatory approval to begin investigating a tidal power project in Alaska.

► The company is also working on a carbon sequestration project with its natural gas reserves in Australia and has invested in BrightSource Energy, which is developing solar technology.

REASONS TO BE BEARISH

► Chevron faces strong competition from Exxon Mobil, BP, ConocoPhillips, and Royal Dutch Shell.

► Like all other oil companies, it is subject to the inherent risks and volatility of the oil and gas market, including fluctuating oil prices, geopolitical risks, weather-related issues, and spills.

► Because Chevron is located in California, it could also face tighter environmental regulations and mandates than other oil companies because of that state's active involvement in passing environmental legislation.

WHAT TO WATCH FOR   All of Chevron's renewable energy demonstration projects bear watching. However, investors should assign the most prominence to (and watch for news about) its biofuels initiative, the expansion of its geothermal capacity, the carbon sequestration project in Australia, and the tidal wave project in Alaska.

CONCLUSION   Bullish. By no stretch of the imagination can Chevron be considered a pure cleantech investment, given its near total reliance on oil and gas for its revenues and profit. But the company's involvement and investment in so many cleantech projects suggests that its interest is more than a public-relations move. Investors who are comfortable investing in a traditional energy company that has the potential to grow into a larger, more formidable cleantech competition over the next ten years are encouraged to consider its stock. With a price-to-earnings ratio of 10, there are few other companies with this level of involvement in the renewable energy field that are so affordable.

GE	COMPANY	General Electric
	SYMBOL	GE
	TRADING MARKET	NYSE
	ADDRESS	3135 Easton Turnpike Fairfield, CT 06828
	PHONE	203-373-2211
	CEO	Jeffrey Immelt
	WEB	*www.ge.com*

DESCRIPTION   General Electric is the world's largest company with a market capitalization of $400 billion. It has eleven separate operating segments and manufactures everything from jet engines to home appliances. Over half of the company's revenue comes from its financial services division, and it also owns the NBC/Universal broadcasting system. It is, however, the company's Energy division that makes GE a true cleantech company. In 2005, CEO Jeff Immelt launched the company's Ecomagination initiative and announced that it would be increasing its investments in cleantech from $700 million to $1.5 billion by 2010. The bulk of this money is expected to be invested in coal gasification, wind, solar, and fuel cell technologies.

REASONS TO BE BULLISH

► GE's Energy division increased its revenue from $16 billion in 2005 to $19 billion in 2006. It expects this figure to increase to over $25 billion by 2008.

► The company is diversified across an array of cleantech sectors, including wind power, solar, fuel cell, and biomass; in 2007 it doubled the amount its cleantech venture arm would be investing in renewable energy from $25 million to $50 million.

► The company has invested heavily in clean coal technology (with its Integrated Gasification Combined Cycle [IGCC] system) and the nuclear industry (with its Advanced Boiling Water Reactors). Both technologies could be in greater demand in the event carbon emission regulations are imposed.

► In addition to its $1.5 billion commitment to fund cleantech-related advances, GE's Global Research Lab is also investing heavily in nanotechnology, an area that could lead to additional breakthroughs in stronger, lighter, and more flexible wind turbines, more efficient photovoltaics, and advances in the economical production of hydrogen.

continued

General Electric continued

► GE is working with Ballard Power Systems and A123 Systems to develop light-weight batteries for hybrid fuel cell buses.
► In 2007, GE made two sizable investments in wind power. It now has invested in fifty wind farms with a total capacity of 2,400 MW of wind power.
► The company received an $18 million grant from the U.S. Department of Energy in 2007 to figure out how to integrate solar cells into building materials, and in late 2007 it acquired a minority interest in PrimeStar, Inc., a promising thin-film start-up.
► As a truly global company, GE is well diversified across markets. It is now the leading wind turbine supplier in the United States and has also established a strong presence in China.

REASONS TO BE BEARISH
► The size of the company makes it difficult to deliver extraordinary returns.
► GE now derives over half of its earnings from its financial subsidiaries. While neither a positive nor a negative, what happens in this sector—especially with regard to interest and inflation rates—could easily overshadow progress in the cleantech arena.
► If solar technology emerges as the "first among equals" in alternative energy, GE, as it is presently configured, is not as strongly positioned to compete as it is in the fields of wind power, fuel cells, nuclear, and clean coal.

WHAT TO WATCH FOR   In the event that carbon emissions are subject to environmental restrictions or there is an accident involving nuclear power, those aspects of its business could be very severely damaged. On the positive side, investors are advised to watch for news of breakthrough developments in the area of thin-film photovoltaics. Investors are also encouraged to keep an eye open for the convergence of clean technologies. For instance, solar cells can be used to generate clean water from water filtration systems. With more than 1 billion people suffering from a lack of clean water, such a marriage could lead to a great many more new sales of both GE's solar cells and its water filtration systems.

CONCLUSION   Bullish. GE is well managed and diversified, and its scientific and research staff is among the best in the world. Investors can expect that GE's Energy division will produce an increasingly larger percentage of the company's overall revenues over the next ten years. The company is a safe, conservative way to make an investment in the cleantech field.

GM		
	COMPANY	General Motors
	SYMBOL	GM
	TRADING MARKET	NYSE
	ADDRESS	300 Renaissance Center Detroit, MI 48265-3000
	PHONE	313-556-5000
	CEO	Rick Wagoner
	WEB	*www.gm.com*

DESCRIPTION   General Motors is now the second largest automobile manufacturer (after Toyota), with revenues of about $170 billion. Its brands include Chevrolet, GMC, Pontiac, Buick, Saturn, and the Hummer. In the past few years, the company has expanded the number of vehicles that are capable of using ethanol and, more recently, it has gotten aggressive about investing in better battery technology and fuel cell technology.

REASONS TO BE BULLISH

▶ After years of losses, in 2007 GM's global auto operations posted a profit.

▶ The company has had some success in cutting its overhead costs. It has closed unprofitable plants, offered buyout packages to 34,000 workers, and modified its health care agreement with its union members.

▶ GM has made serious inroads in the China market and could benefit from that country's continued economic expansion.

▶ The company has assigned hundreds of engineers and millions of dollars in an effort to become the greenest company in the auto industry. It even became the first automobile company to support a cap on carbon emissions.

▶ GM now has fifteen vehicles that are ethanol-capable and it has manufactured the Saturn Vue—a hybrid sports utility vehicle.

▶ The GM "Volt," an advanced hybrid vehicle capable of achieving 150 gallons per gallon, is expected to be on the road in 2009.

▶ In mid 2007, GM's research lab turned its hydrogen fuel cell technology over to its engineering group—a sign that the technology is nearing production. In fact, senior GM officials have indicated a fuel cell vehicle will be in production by 2012.

continued

REASONS TO BE BEARISH

► The company is still straddled with huge financial obligations—especially health care and pension costs—and its position in China is likely to be challenged by lower-cost competitors.

► Toyota is currently ahead of GM with regard to hybrid vehicles and battery technology, and it is likely to outpace GM in hybrid sales for the foreseeable future.

► There is no guarantee that GM's aggressive push in advanced hybrid automobiles or fuel cell vehicles will be successful.

► Even if the company's new products are successful, it is possible that union members—and not shareholders—will be the first beneficiaries of any turnaround.

WHAT TO WATCH FOR   All things being equal, General Motors must continue to control its fixed costs and its recent deal with the UAW regarding health care and pension benefits should help. Beyond that, the company's long-term success will be in part dependent upon its ability to sustain its success in China. In terms of becoming a more environmentally friendly company, investors will want to see if the Volt hits the market in 2009 and then monitor how the market reacts to it. Beyond that, GM's push into fuel cell vehicles could very well be what sets it apart from its competitors and allows it to regain its position as the world's largest automobile manufacturer.

CONCLUSION   Bullish. It is easy to be pessimistic about GM's prospects—especially given how it has fared over the past five years—but I believe its large bet on hybrid and fuel cell technology will pay off. To be sure, it is risky but for GM it is not nearly as risky as maintaining the status quo.

GS	COMPANY	Goldman Sachs
	SYMBOL	GS
	TRADING MARKET	NYSE
	ADDRESS	85 Broad Street New York, NY 10004
	PHONE	212-902-1000
	CEO	Lloyd Blankfein
	WEB	*www.gs.com*

DESCRIPTION   Goldman Sachs is one of the world's leading investment banks and it provides banking, securities, and management services to corporations, financial institutions, governments, and high-net-worth individuals. It is listed as a cleantech company because in 2005 it became the first financial institution to release an environmental policy framework and then backed up its pledge with a commitment to invest over $1 billion in renewable energy companies.

REASONS TO BE BULLISH
► Goldman Sachs is extremely profitable. Its profits for 2007 were 76 percent higher than the previous year.
► In 2007, it sold its stake in Horizon Wind Energy to Energias de Portugal for $2.9 billion. Much of this money can be expected to be redirected into other alternative energy investments.
► The company has a large private equity investment in SunEdison, a Baltimore-based solar photovoltaic company, and it is also heavily invested in First Solar, a leading solar cell manufacturer.
► The company has arranged $217 million in debt financing for Northeast Biofuels; made a $30 million investment in Iogen, an early-stage cellulosic ethanol producer; and owns an undisclosed percentage of Nordex, a wind turbine manufacturer.
► In 2007, Goldman Sachs purchased a 10 percent stake in the United Kingdom conglomerate Climate Exchange, Plc. The deal is in response to the expectation that governments will soon begin placing restrictions on carbon emissions and that the marketplace will need to construct a trading system—along the lines of the Climate Exchange—to facilitate the trading of carbon credits.

continued

► The company now expects all of its analysts to incorporate environmental data into investment research.

REASONS TO BE BEARISH
► Goldman Sachs faces increased competition from other investment banks. In the past year Bank of America has announced it will create a $20 billion initiative to support renewable energy, and Merrill Lynch has initiated a $3 billion program.
► The company may suffer from negative publicity from supporting companies and/or industries that don't have a positive environmental image, such as the coal industry.
► Due to Goldman Sachs's other businesses, it has some exposure to the sub-prime mortgage market and its stock could be adversely affected by a worsening of that situation.

WHAT TO WATCH FOR   When Goldman Sachs—one of the world's leading banks—indicated that it intended to invest in renewable energy, it served as a wake-up call for the rest of Wall Street. Investors are encouraged to monitor its actions, if for no other reason than whatever it does, other investing houses are likely to follow suit. To this end, if the company turns bearish on coal it could be a strong indicator that other renewable energy sources will have to increase output in order to cover the demand.

CONCLUSION   Bullish. Goldman Sachs is a solid, low-risk investment. Investors looking to add some diversity to their portfolio in the field of financial services, while at the same time playing the cleantech market, are wise to consider an investment in the company.

IBM	COMPANY	IBM
	SYMBOL	IBM
	TRADING MARKET	NYSE
	ADDRESS	1133 Westchester Avenue White Plains, NY 10604
	PHONE	800-IBM-4YOU
	CEO	Sam Palmisano
	WEB	*www.ibm.com*

DESCRIPTION   IBM is the biggest computer equipment vendor and information technology provider in the world and has a rich history of creating, developing, and manufacturing advanced information technologies, including highly energy-efficient computer chips. In 2007, the company unveiled its Big Green Innovations program and signaled that it viewed cleantech as a new business niche.

REASONS TO BE BULLISH
▶ With its state-of-the-art research laboratories, a $7 billion annual research and development budget, and a team of world-class scientists, IBM is well positioned to develop a variety of cutting-edge clean technologies, such as new energy-efficient materials and advances in photovoltaics.
▶ IBM has a rich history of using technology to expand existing markets and create new ones. For instance, as a leader in sensor, RFID, and software technology, IBM can help businesses save a great deal of money by minimizing energy costs. To this end, the company is aggressively pursuing opportunities in the field of "smart networks," which help businesses better control their energy usage by giving them real-time feedback on pricing.
▶ As a leader in the field of supercomputing, IBM can harness the power of these machines for its own competitive advantage. For example, supercomputers can be used to model new energy-saving materials or predict better ways for companies to reduce energy costs. The computers can also be used to facilitate the creation of new biofuels.

continued

► As a leader in the development of carbon nanotubes and nanotechnology research, IBM could be well positioned for future growth to the extent that these super-strong, super-light, and extremely conductive materials become an important component of future computer chips and next-generation thin-film solar cells.

► As an established consulting company, IBM's consultants are well positioned to stay abreast of the latest advances in cleantech and thus help other businesses take advantage of these advances.

REASONS TO BE BEARISH

► Because it is one of the world's largest companies, it is unlikely that IBM will experience rapid growth.

► Also because of its size, questions linger as to whether IBM will be nimble enough to react and take advantage of new opportunities in the cleantech space as they emerge.

WHAT TO WATCH FOR   To the extent that businesses and residences begin to intelligently employ networks of sensors to monitor and manage energy usage, IBM, as a leader in many of the enabling technologies (RFID, sensors, etc.), will be well positioned to profit from this transition. Investors should keep an eye on IBM's race with Intel to develop the most energy-efficient computer chip. Computers will continue to suck up an increasing amount of energy for the foreseeable future, and whichever company can produce the most "output per watt" should be able to generate a substantial amount of revenue.

CONCLUSION   Bullish. Although IBM is not a cleantech company per se, by virtue of its size and technological strength it will be a player in this space. The company is well positioned to benefit from the continued and growing interest in renewable energy because it has its fingers in almost every sector of the environmental pie.

Fortune **500 companies**

PCG	COMPANY	PG&E Corporation
	SYMBOL	PCG
	TRADING MARKET	NYSE
	ADDRESS	One Market Spear Tower, Suite 2400 San Francisco, CA 94105
	PHONE	415-267-7070
	CEO	Peter A. Darbee
	WEB	*www.pgecorp.com*

DESCRIPTION   PG&E Corporation is the owner of the Pacific Gas & Electric Company, a regulated utility servicing 13 million people in Northern and Central California. The utility has businesses in electricity and natural gas distribution; electricity generation, procurement, and transmission; and natural gas procurement, transportation, and storage. It is listed as a cleantech company because 13 percent of its electricity is currently produced from renewable energy sources, and that figure is expected to increase to 20 percent by 2010.

REASONS TO BE BULLISH

► Among all utilities, PG&E produces the most electricity from renewable resources.

► In addition to deriving 13 percent from renewable resources, the company generated another 46 percent of its electricity from nuclear power and hydroelectric power. This means that nearly 60 percent of all of its energy emits no carbon dioxide. In the event the state of California or the federal government imposes limits on carbon dioxide emissions, PG&E could be a bigger winner.

► The company sports a reasonable price-to-earnings ratio, projects healthy growth through 2010, and resides in a well-regulated environment. This makes PG&E a relatively low-risk investment.

► The company is aggressively pursuing a variety of renewable energy projects, including projects in the following areas: geothermal, wind, solar, fuel cell, biomass, and wave power.

continued

► PG&E has indicated that it plans to install 9.3 million "smart meters" in its customers' homes and businesses, and, by reducing energy usage, this could help keep the company from needing to build as many as five new coal-fired power plants.

REASONS TO BE BEARISH

► The company has experienced healthy growth over the past five years and it currently trades at a premium to some of its industry peers.

WHAT TO WATCH FOR   While the majority of its renewable energy projects remain small, a number of them hold great potential. To this end, the company is considering building a transmission line that could import between 1,500 and 3,000 MW of wind-generated power by 2011. Also, initiatives in the area of fuel-cell-generated power, such as the one it undertook with Starwood Hotels, bear watching—if other large businesses also begin transitioning to fuel cell plants, it could portend a switch to that energy source. In the mid-term, investors are encouraged to watch how many customers begin switching to solar power and whether a proposed 120 MW geothermal facility in Oregon becomes operational within the next few years. Longer term, PG&E's biomass and wave power projects bear watching, as does a pilot project it is undertaking to review the feasibility of storing excess electricity in hybrid plug-in vehicles. (The idea is to recharge the batteries of the automobiles in the evening, when the price of electricity is low, and use the batteries to power homes and businesses during the peak hours when electricity is more expensive.)

CONCLUSION   Bullish. It is not accurate to call PG&E a pure cleantech investment, but for investors looking for a safe, low-risk investment in a company that is aggressively pursuing renewable energy, PG&E is a solid investment.

SI	COMPANY	Siemens AG
	SYMBOL	SI
	TRADING MARKET	NYSE
	ADDRESS	Wittelsbacherplatz 2 Munich, 80333 Germany
	PHONE	49-89-636-32474
	CEO	Peter Loescher
	WEB	*www.siemens.com*

DESCRIPTION   Like its American counterpart General Electric, Siemens AG is a massive, well-diversified conglomerate that is involved in everything from trains to lighting. It has positions in communications, industrial automation, power generation, medical diagnostics, rail transportation systems, automotive electronics, and lighting. It is considered a "cleantech" company because its positions in power generation (12 percent), power transmission and distribution (7 percent), building technologies (5.5 percent), and lighting (5 percent) represent almost one-third of the company's value.

REASONS TO BE BULLISH

► As a multinational corporation with a strong presence in Europe, the Middle East, Asia, and the United States, Siemens is well positioned to benefit from the global increase in the demand for clean energy.

► Additionally, Siemens is well diversified across various cleantech sectors with positions in wind power, instrumentation and controls, gas turbine power plants, fuel cell technology, wave power, and ethanol plant construction.

► Since 2000, Siemens has supplied process automation systems on two-thirds of the fuel ethanol plants built in the United States. The company now estimates that the plants it has supplied are providing over 2 billion gallons of ethanol annually. As the industry continues to expand, Siemens will benefit.

► Siemens is well positioned to benefit from the growing demand in wind power. With more than twenty-five years of experience in the wind industry and with a wide array of products that serve both on- and offshore wind farms, the company has already installed more than 6,000 wind turbines, and in 2006 it opened a large manufacturing facility in Iowa to meet the growing demand for wind turbines in the United States.

continued

► In 2007, the company continued to generate a profit and its price-to-earnings ratio was approximately 15—which means that it trades at a slight discount to its leading industry peer, General Electric.

► Siemens has more than thirty years of research and development experience in the field of solid-oxide fuel cells. As the fuel cell industry grows, Siemens should expand along with it.

► Over the past few years, the company has made great strides in improving the efficiency of lighting. Its work in the area of light-emitting diodes could extend the environmental benefits beyond what even the newer compact fluorescent lamps are achieving.

► In 2005, the company purchased Wavegen and began positioning itself to participate in the emerging field of wave power.

REASONS TO BE BEARISH

► In mid-2007, in the wake of a serious investigation concerning whether the company used multi-million-dollar bribes to win some telecommunications contracts, the company hired a new CEO. The investigation is likely to cloud the company's prospects for some time.

WHAT TO WATCH FOR   Since the company is not limited to cleantech, it is important for investors to understand that its stock will be driven in large part by its progress in areas unrelated to cleantech, such as communications and medical diagnostics.

CONCLUSION   Bullish. Siemens is not a pure-play cleantech investment but for investors looking for a safe and conservative way to play the cleantech field, it is a wise investment choice. The company trades at a reasonable valuation (a P/E ratio of 15) and has a sizable presence in ethanol, wind, and fuel cell industries.

Conclusion

As the preceding pages documented, all of the *Fortune* 500 companies profiled are engaged in activities that transcend cleantech. In fact, for most of the companies, renewable energy represents just a modest percentage of their overall business. Nevertheless, the sheer size of these companies often means that even a small percentage can translate into a multi-billion-dollar business enterprise. And this implies that in terms of revenues and profits, these *Fortune* 500 companies are—in dollar terms alone—among the largest cleantech companies in the world.

Undoubtedly, some investors will be inclined not to invest in these large companies for any number of reasons, including their opposition to the company's involvement in more traditional (and polluting) energy sources. Others perhaps will shy away from investment because they do not believe that these companies, owing to their large sizes, will be able to offer the same type of returns as some of the smaller and mid-size companies. (On the flip side, though, these large companies are also likely to be less volatile than their smaller counterparts.)

The decision to invest or not in these companies is, of course, a personal one, but investors who choose to ignore this option and instead focus on pure-play ethanol, wind, or solar companies must still pay attention to these large companies. The larger entities will remain competitors to many of the smaller cleantech companies, and could thus have a considerable impact on the fortunes of many of the pure-play companies.

"We've got the tree-huggers, the do-gooders, the sod-busters, the cheap hawks, the evangelicals and Willy Nelson in favor of biofuels."

—James Woolsey, former CIA Director

Chapter Four

Biofuels: Fuel of the Future?

For many Americans there is no more glaring symbol of everything that is wrong with our current energy alternatives than that most ubiquitous of commodities: gasoline. Not only are we reminded of its impact on our pocketbooks every time we visit the gas pump, we often see (and smell) the connection between the fuel and global climate change whenever a bus, truck, or older car belches out a cloud of black smoke. Still others are apt to note our reliance on the stuff and draw a connection to the United States' continued military presence in the Middle East.

Regardless of the intellectual, scientific, or political merits of these various opinions, it is true that most Americans want to reduce our reliance on oil, and over the past few years there have been increasing calls for "energy independence" from politicians, business leaders, and citizens alike. As a result, there has been a lot more attention paid to creating more environmentally friendly alternatives.

The most prominent of these alternatives is ethanol. In 2007, just a year after proclaiming that America was "addicted to oil," President Bush called upon Congress and the American people to increase ethanol production from its present level of 12 billion gallons to 35 billion gallons by 2017.

This call, in combination with consumers' economic and environmental concerns about gas, has spurred a rash of ethanol IPOs and led Clean Edge Research to estimate that the ethanol market will quadruple from $20 billion in 2006 to over $80 billion by 2016. These factors have also caught the attention of some heavy hitters, including Microsoft chairman Bill Gates, whose money management firm has invested $84 million in Pacific Ethanol, and Virgin Group chairman Richard Branson, who has indicated that he will invest up to $3 billion in renewable fuels.

With all this public attention, it is only natural that individual investor interest has also been piqued. Alas, ethanol's growth is just one side of the biofuels story. Before investing in this space, investors need to familiarize themselves with ethanol's shortcomings as well as its many formidable competitors.

When thinking of ethanol, it is useful to recall that old quote about democracy by Winston Churchill: "It is the worst form of government, except for all the others." In essence, he was saying that for all of its problems, democracy was still better than all of the other alternatives. For the time being, ethanol can be thought of in much the same manner with regard to other biofuels, primarily because it is more abundant and currently easier to produce. But unlike democracy, ethanol's staying power as "the least worst" form of biofuel is more suspect.

For starters, much of its current success can be attributed to the generous government subsidies ethanol production has received over the past years. Unfortunately, ethanol remains a poor substitute for gasoline.

Second, it is nowhere near being cost competitive with gasoline and must therefore still rely heavily on a 51-cent tax credit. If this were to go away, the impact on the industry would be devastating. (It is worth noting that ethanol can be price-competitive with gasoline, but the feedstock that is best able to do this at the present time is sugar cane, and only Brazil has a large enough supply.)

Part of ethanol's problem stems from the fact that it has a high water content. This means that it can't be shipped via pipelines and must instead be distributed via railcars and trucks. But even if the price were competitive, ethanol would still suffer from another serious problem: only 1,000 of the more than 170,000 fuel stations in America are presently equipped to sell the stuff. (This situation, I should add, is exacerbated by oil and gas companies, which are not exactly rushing to resolve the issue.)

Third, ethanol is not nearly as environmentally friendly as many proponents would have people believe. At the current time, it takes roughly seven gallons of gasoline to produce ten gallons of ethanol.

Ethanol is made even less attractive because it has a lower net energy value than gasoline. Put another way, when you fill up your tank with ethanol you will deplete your tank 20 to 30 percent sooner than if you used regular gasoline. Therefore, although ethanol is often less expensive than gas (thanks again to the generous subsidies it receives) it is not quite the bargain that a straight price comparison at the filling station might lead one to expect.

Proponents of ethanol will argue that it is still more environmentally friendly than gasoline. While this is true, again, the story is not nearly as compelling when one considers that most ethanol plants are fueled by either natural gas or coal and thus emit a good deal of carbon dioxide in the production process. Ethanol's environmental advantage is further minimized after we take into consideration the costs associated with fertilizing the corn crop, harvesting it, and ultimately transporting the final product to its various destinations.

A fifth problem with corn-produced ethanol is the corn itself. As demand for ethanol has increased, the price of corn has sky-rocketed—from just under $2 a bushel in 2006 to nearly $4 a bushel in early 2007. The impact has been dramatic. Not only have ethanol prices increased and profit margins been squeezed, the costs of a variety of other corn-related food products have increased as well. In addition to adversely impacting beef and dairy farmers who rely on corn to feed their livestock, consumers have also been hit with higher grocery bills.

This problem is likely to get worse before it gets better because of another factor that investors need to be aware of: ethanol supply is burgeoning. As of mid-2007, more than eighty new ethanol plants were under construction. The net effect, in the short run, will be a classic demand versus supply problem.

Unfortunately, the laws of supply and demand may end up working against ethanol producers in two ways. First, the higher price of corn will depress profit margins, and then the possibility that ethanol supply will exceed demand could depress the price at the pump.

Proponents of ethanol will counter that in the long run the market will be able to absorb all of the ethanol that is produced. And in a way they are correct, but this only serves to highlight another problem. It has been estimated that even if all the corn in the United States went into the production of ethanol, the country could only replace 12 percent of the gasoline market.

The problem could be somewhat relieved by importing cheaper ethanol from Brazil, but the U.S. government currently imposes a 54-cent-per-gallon tariff on ethanol imports in order to protect U.S. ethanol producers.

The New Kid on the Block: Cellulosic Ethanol

Consumers interested in biofuels should focus on the reality of ethanol's limited capacity. Ethanol could still have a promising future, but for the reasons just elucidated, it is unlikely to be corn-produced ethanol that will lead the way.

As it stands, producers today can squeeze about 420 gallons of ethanol out of an acre of corn. More efficient distillation techniques, better catalysts, and even genetically enhanced corn might be able to increase this amount to 750 gallons per acre, but even then ethanol could only replace 20 percent of the current fuel market.

One long-term solution might be the production of cellulosic ethanol. Cellulosic ethanol is chemically identical to corn ethanol, but instead of being produced from the kernel of corn, the ethanol is produced from lignocellulose, a structural material that composes much of the mass of many agricultural products including corn stover, switchgrass, oat, wheat, barley straw, and even wood sources.

The potential advantages of cellulosic ethanol are many. For starters, the feedstock sources are more distributed and plentiful. Whereas corn is mostly grown in the Midwest, cellulosic feedstocks can be found virtually everywhere. One company, Range Fuels, for instance, is constructing a cellulosic ethanol plant in Georgia to take advantage of an abundant supply of wood and other forest products. This means that the production of ethanol could take place much closer to where the fuel will actually be used, thus eliminating costly and unnecessary transportation costs.

Through a combination of other advances, it is also feasible that farmers will learn to produce more biomass per acre. (Biomass refers to both living and recently dead biological matter, such as switchgrass, wood, and sugarcane, which can be used as fuel or for industrial production.) This, in turn, has led some experts to speculate that in a few decades it might be possible to get as many as 2,700 gallons of ethanol per acre from various feedstocks.

Cellulosic ethanol, however, is unlikely to take decades before it becomes competitive with corn ethanol. Vinod Khosla, a venture capitalist who has made numerous investments in the field, has publicly said that he believes cellulosic ethanol will be competitive with corn ethanol as early as 2009.

If so, a number of today's leading ethanol producers will need to make plans to transition to cellulosic ethanol. Converting the facilities to handle a feedstock other than corn is not particularly problematic; what is more worrisome is that a number of the current ethanol plants have been strategically located in proximity to corn. If corn is no longer the primary feedstock, though, those facilities—and the companies that operate them—could be adversely affected.

Investors' dilemma regarding ethanol won't end with a transition to cellulosic ethanol. A number of private start-ups profiled in this chapter are now devising radically different methods of producing cellulosic ethanol. Range Fuels, for instance, is developing a thermochemical process; Iogen is seeking to create new enzymes that more efficiently extract sugars from wheat and straw and convert it into ethanol; and Mascoma is seeking to employ microbes to aid in the ethanol conversion process. Which technology will win in the commercial marketplace is the subject of fierce debate and, at this time, there is no clear indication of how things will shake out.

And the Contenders

Nor is there any real indication that ethanol—be it either corn-based or cellulosic—will be the biofuel of the future. ADM and Imperium Renewables are making sizable bets that biodiesel will be the big biofuel winner for five reasons: 1) it is being produced today; 2) it has a significantly higher net energy value than ethanol or even regular gasoline; 3) it is cleaner than both ethanol and regular diesel and will benefit from new regulations imposed by the EPA mandating that all diesel fuels generate fewer sulfur emissions; 4) it can be distributed via today's infrastructure of pipelines; and 5) it can be used in existing diesel vehicles. Ethanol, on the other hand, can be used in existing automobiles only in low blends and it requires cars to be modified to handle higher blends.

Another biofuel that could do extremely well is biobutanol. The advantage of biobutanol, which is currently under development by DuPont and BP, is that it can be manufactured from cornstarch or sugar beets, and its properties are more like gasoline. This means that it has a higher net energy density than either ethanol or biodiesel, and it can be transported using the existing gasoline infrastructure.

Of course, other possibilities exist as well. One is that entirely new technologies will be developed to create fuel sources in unique and innovative ways. One intriguing technology, being pursued by GreenFuel Technologies, includes the possibility that algae might be used to consume or "eat" carbon dioxide. The algae can then be reused as a carbon energy source. A second alternative is synthetic biology. Synthetic Genomics, for instance, is working to create "designer bacteria" that could create a simple, low-cost method of producing various biofuels and even hydrogen.

To this latter point, investors must also be open to the long-term possibility that hydrogen might be the fuel source of the future. This idea will be explored in greater detail in Chapter Seven, but it is worth mentioning here that every major automobile manufacturer is currently exploring fuel cell technology. In 2007, General Motors announced it was shifting more than 500 of its research and development scientists over to the production side of the company to help design and build fuel cell vehicles. Many analysts feel this act was a clear sign that the technology may be closer to the commercial marketplace than has been generally accepted.

Of course, another possibility is that dramatic advances in engine design or battery technology could yield improvements in gas mileage so significant that the need for biofuels might well be mitigated.

The biggest variable in the development of biofuels, however, is government involvement. I have already mentioned how the 51-cent tax credit and the 54-cent tariff on ethanol imports have helped the corn ethanol industry grow over the past few years, but it is worth noting that the government is now investing $385 million in cellulosic ethanol research and development and another $125 million in synthetic biology for the creation of new biofuels.

The federal government is also likely to influence the biofuels market through the regulations that it imposes. For instance, the EPA's new rules on sulfur emissions have been a boon to biodiesel production, and similar mandates on the percentage of ethanol that must be blended with gasoline could go a long way toward determining how large the ethanol industry grows. Bottom line: As the government goes, so will the biofuel industry go.

With that introduction, let's look at some of the most promising ethanol, cellulosic ethanol, and other biofuel companies.

Biofuel Companies

ABG	COMPANY	Abengoa Bioenergy (a subsidiary of Abengoa)
	SYMBOL	ABG
	TRADING MARKET	Various European stock exchanges
	ADDRESS	1400 Elbridge Payne Road, Suite 212 Chesterfield, MO 63017
	PHONE	636-728-0508
	CEO	Javier Salgado
	WEB	*www.abengoabioenergy.com*

DESCRIPTION   Abengoa Bioenergy is dedicated to the development of biofuels. Operating through different subsidiaries, the company owns and operates a variety of facilities for producing and marketing bioethanol throughout the United States and Europe.

REASONS TO BE BULLISH

► At the present time, Abengoa is the largest ethanol producer in Europe and the fifth largest in the United States. It produces over 1 billion gallons of ethanol annually.

► In 2007, the company received a $76 million grant from the U.S. Department of Energy to develop a pilot plant for the production of cellulosic ethanol.

► In the area of corn ethanol production, Abengoa claims to have developed a technology that achieves a very high conversion rate for converting cornstarch into sugar. If true, it is the type of development that should allow Abengoa to be more profitable than other ethanol producers.

► In 2006, the company signed a cooperative agreement with Ford Motor Company to develop "flexible fuel" engines for Ford's line of automobiles in Spain to use bioethanol E85 manufactured by Abengoa Bioenergy.

► Abengoa Bioenergy is just one component of Abengoa. The company has a strong research and development team, and it also has cleantech-related businesses in the areas of solar, environmental services, industrial engineering and construction, and information technologies; it is thus a more diversified investment than a typical bioethanol company.

continued

► Abengoa is geographically diverse. It does 44 percent of its business in Spain, 28 percent in Latin America, 11 percent in Europe, and 10 percent in the United States.

REASONS TO BE BEARISH

► The company's new cellulosic ethanol plant will cost $300 million to construct and will not be operational until 2010.

► In the cellulosic ethanol field, Abengoa will face considerable competitive pressure from companies such as Iogen, Cilion, Range Fuels, and BlueFire Ethanol. In the corn ethanol business, it will face stiff competition from ADM, Aventine Renewable Energy, and POET.

► In the company's other businesses (e.g. solar, construction, environmental services) it will also face competition; however, the greater danger may be that it will be difficult for management to operate the company's diverse components as a cohesive unit given the unique demands of each division.

WHAT TO WATCH FOR   To prosper over the long term, Abengoa will need to grow its bioenergy and solar divisions. Currently, the two components represent less than 20 percent of its overall business. Investors should look for news that Abengoa's new cellulosic plant will be operational by 2010. If it is producing at least 100 million gallons of ethanol annually by that time, it will be a bullish sign.

CONCLUSION   Neutral. The diversity of Abengoa's other renewable energy divisions makes it an attractive cleantech play; however, until it bolsters both its bioethanol and solar businesses, investors should treat the stock with caution. If management decides to spin off its industrial engineering, information technologies, or environmental services, it will be easier to evaluate the value of the company. If this occurs, many of its cleantech businesses might make solid investments.

Biofuel Companies

ADM	COMPANY	Archer Daniels Midland
	SYMBOL	ADM
	TRADING MARKET	NYSE
	ADDRESS	4666 Faries Parkway Decatur, IL 62526
	PHONE	800-637-5843
	CEO	Patricia Woertz
	WEB	*www.admworld.com*

DESCRIPTION ADM bills itself as "supermarket to the world." While it is the leading ethanol producer in the United States—and as such can be seen as a cleantech company—it is also a global agricultural leader and is in the business of procuring, transporting, storing, processing, and marketing a wide range of agricultural products, including oilseeds, corn, wheat, and cocoa. Ethanol makes up only about 20 percent of its business. ADM is primarily a powerhouse in food and beverage additives.

REASONS TO BE BULLISH
▶ The company has been consistently profitable over its long history, and there is little to suggest that it won't continue this trend in 2008 and beyond. Global demand for both food and bioenergy is increasing and the company is well positioned to benefit from both trends.
▶ Its diversified product portfolio and access to global markets protects it well from wild fluctuations that are common to other smaller, ethanol producers.
▶ ADM expects to increase ethanol production by 500 million gallons by 2009, bringing its total to 1.7 billion gallons.
▶ The company has the financial resources to engage in cutting-edge research and development, and with its access to vast amounts of agricultural products other than corn, it could easily become a leader in the production of cellulosic ethanol.
▶ Over the past five years, the company has spent $3.4 billion on new plants and facilities. These investments will help ensure that it stays competitive.
▶ In 2006, it announced plans to begin building a 50-million-gallon plant for biodiesel.

continued

REASONS TO BE BEARISH
- ➤ ADM is not a pure-play cleantech investment. It is a food-production company, and its stock is subject to fluctuation depending on weather-related issues and geopolitical concerns.
- ➤ Ethanol production (and supply) could easily outpace demand and, if combined with lower oil prices, the combination could have an adverse impact on ethanol's margins.

WHAT TO WATCH FOR   The price of ethanol is closely tied to the price of oil, so investors should closely monitor the price of the latter. To the extent that oil increases, ethanol will become more attractive. Investors are also encouraged to monitor government subsidies to ethanol. Although government support is unlikely to erode anytime soon, federal budget deficit-related pressures could cause Congress to revisit the large incentives it provides to the ethanol industry. Longer term, investors will want to look for news of progress on cellulosic ethanol production. Abengoa Bioenergy is building a massive 1.3-billion-gallon cellulosic facility in Spain that could hurt ADM in European markets, and private start-ups such as Iogen and Mascoma might disrupt ADM's ethanol business in the long run.

CONCLUSION   Bullish. Although ADM is by no means a pure-play cleantech investment, it is well positioned to benefit from the growing expansion of both the ethanol and biodiesel markets. Provided the company's stock price is trading within thirteen and eighteen times its price-to-earnings ratio, it remains a solid investment.

COMPANY	Amyris Biotechnologies
INVESTORS	Khosla Ventures, Kleiner Perkins Caufield & Byers, and Texas Pacific Group Ventures
ADDRESS	5980 Horton Street, Suite 450 Emeryville, CA 94608
PHONE	510-450-0761
CEO	John Melo
WEB	*www.amyrisbiotech.com*

DESCRIPTION Amyris Biotechnologies is a development-stage biotechnology company employing synthetic biology in a fermentation process that uses custom-designed microbes to produce high-performance biofuels that are cost-effective, renewable, and compatible with current automotive and distribution technologies. (Also, in an area that isn't related to cleantech, the company is hoping to use synthetic biology to manufacture a microbe that can recreate a complex molecule that is found in only limited quantities in the natural world, but is highly effective at treating malaria—a disease that kills over 1 million people annually.)

WHY IT IS DISRUPTIVE By isolating genes from their natural sources and inserting them into industrial microbes, Amyris is hoping to produce a series of complex molecules that have a higher net energy density than ethanol and to do so in a manner that is stable, scalable, and cost-effective. If Amyris is successful, it could not only pioneer a significantly cheaper and more efficient method of producing biodiesel it could serve a much larger market because its biofuels are based on hydrocarbons—meaning they could easily operate in regular car engines without needing any retrofitting. The company has raised $20 million from two of Silicon Valley's best-known venture capitalists—John Doerr and Vinod Khosla—and hired an experienced CEO, John Melo. He formerly served as president of U.S. Fuel Operations for BP.

continued

WHAT TO WATCH FOR   In addition to making enzymes that are optimized for breaking biomass down for cellulose, the company will need to demonstrate that its technology is scalable. To this end, signs that it is moving forward with a manufacturing facility will be a bullish indicator. Interested parties should monitor the status of its pilot plant which is expected to be operational in 2009 and producing large quantities by 2010. The company is also partnering with Virgin Airlines to manufacture a bio-friendly jet fuel. At the present time, it is one of only a few companies pursuing this lucrative niche—jet fuel currently contributes 12 percent of the carbon dioxide emissions into the environment—but if it can develop such a fuel, that will be a very bullish indicator.

CONCLUSION   Neutral. Amyris Biotechnologies is a private company and will likely not go public for some time. In the event that it does, investors are encouraged to discern how its technology is different from Synthetic Genomics' technology and then discern which company is closest to commercial production.

Biofuel Companies

ANDE	COMPANY	The Andersons Inc.
	SYMBOL	ANDE
	TRADING MARKET	NASDAQ
	ADDRESS	480 W. Dussel Drive Maumee, OH 43537
	PHONE	419-893-5050
	CEO	Michael J. Anderson
	WEB	*www.andersonsinc.com*

DESCRIPTION The Andersons Inc. is a diversified agricultural and transportation company with interests in the grain, ethanol, and plant nutrient sectors, as well as railcar marketing, industrial products manufacturing, and general merchandise retailing.

REASONS TO BE BULLISH

► Andersons is profitable and in 2006 generated a profit of $28 million on sales of $1.5 billion—an increase over 2005 figures, which had the company generating a profit of only $12 million on sales of $1.2 billion. In mid-2007, the company raised full-year earnings per share from $2.60 to $3.05.

► Andersons is continuing to grow its ethanol business and brought a new plant online during the first half of 2007.

► The company has a strong balance sheet and has the necessary financial resources to fund additional ethanol plant expansion.

► Because the company's Rail Group and Plant Nutrient Group are quite sizable—2006 revenues were $113 million and $265 million, respectively—it is not nearly as vulnerable to the cyclical fluctuations of the ethanol business as others in the field.

► Andersons has consistently provided shareholders with a regular, albeit modest, dividend.

► As a result of its experience managing corn, Andersons appears better equipped than some other smaller ethanol producers to handle the volatile nature of the commodity.

continued

REASONS TO BE BEARISH

► The company's stock had quite a run up in price in 2006 as a result of investor interest in ethanol, and it has since receded. It is possible that the stock will continue to drop until its price-to-earnings ratio is more in line with other companies that have similar diversified interests. ADM, for example, historically trades at an average PE ratio of 16.

WHAT TO WATCH FOR   Andersons has grown steadily for the past seven years. Investors should be careful that the company doesn't overexpand into the ethanol business. They should also keep an eye open for news that the company is expanding into other biofuels such as cellulosic ethanol or biodiesel. Both would be positive signs. In the event of consolidation within the ethanol industry, look for Andersons to acquire some of the smaller, less profitable ethanol facilities.

CONCLUSION   Bullish. The company's strong past performance, diversified nature, and plans for additional growth bode well for its future performance. At the time of this writing, its price still appears a little high when compared with historical averages but investors are encouraged to consider the stock if its trades at a PE ratio below 17.

Biofuel Companies

AVR	COMPANY	Aventine Renewable Energy Holdings
	SYMBOL	AVR
	TRADING MARKET	NYSE
	ADDRESS	1300 South 2nd Street Pekin, IL 61555-0010
	PHONE	309-347-9200
	CEO	Ronald H. Miller
	WEB	*www.aventinerei.com*

DESCRIPTION   Aventine Renewable Energy produces and markets ethanol, and this aspect of its business represents 96 percent of its total revenue. It also has a smaller business producing various coproducts, such as distillers' grain, corn gluten feed, and brewer's yeast. In 2006, the company sold almost 700 million gallons of ethanol—approximately 13 percent of the total sold in the United States.

REASONS TO BE BULLISH

► The company is profitable, and in 2006 its revenue increased 70 percent.

► As a leading marketer of ethanol, it has well-established relationships with companies including Royal Dutch Shell, ConocoPhillips, Exxon Mobil, and Chevron.

► Aventine's unique distribution infrastructure allows it to better play the corn market to take advantage of ethanol pricing. (For instance, in a depressed market the company can store more ethanol and in a seller's market it can more quickly reduce its inventory.)

► A new 57-million-gallon facility came online in early 2007, and the company expects to expand production at its other locations.

► In March of 2007, Aventine entered the biodiesel marketing business.

REASONS TO BE BEARISH

► Although Aventine markets a great deal of ethanol, it produces only about 200 million gallons of ethanol itself. It is, therefore, dependent on maintaining relationships with the leading oil companies and must continue to establish new ones in order to keep its business growing. In 2007, VeraSun Energy ceased its relationship with the company.

continued

► The company's expansion plans are modest compared with its leading competitors.

WHAT TO WATCH FOR   Aventine will need to continue to expand its ethanol production as well as increase the total number of gallons of ethanol it is marketing to continue to stay abreast of competitors such as VeraSun and US BioEnergy. Alternatively, it will need to begin acquiring smaller, less competitive ethanol companies. Investors are also encouraged to watch for progress in the area of biodiesel. The company's ability to market both biodiesel and ethanol could give it a competitive advantage over competitors that market only ethanol.

CONCLUSION   Bearish. While Aventine does have some strength in the area of distribution, it will need to bolster its ethanol production in order to be a long-term player. If the company begins acquiring ethanol production facilities from less competitive producers, investors might want to revisit an investment.

Biofuel Companies

BIOF	COMPANY	BioFuel Energy
	SYMBOL	BIOF
	TRADING MARKET	NASDAQ
	ADDRESS	1801 Broadway, Suite 1060 Denver, CO 80202
	PHONE	303-592-8110
	CEO	Thomas J. Edelman
	WEB	*www.bfenergy.com*

DESCRIPTION BioFuel Energy is a development-stage ethanol company that has two 115-million-gallon-a-year production facilities under development in Wood River, Nebraska, and Fairmont, Minnesota. It has also acquired the land and received regulatory approval to begin construction of three other 115-million-gallon facilities. When complete, BioFuel Energy will be among the larger ethanol producers.

REASONS TO BE BULLISH
► BioFuel Energy is backed by Cargill. This relationship could help it significantly as it attempts to break into the competitive world of ethanol production. Cargill is expected to help BioFuel with corn procurement, ethanol distribution, and byproduct sales. All three should help improve the company's margins.
► BioFuel should be able to execute on its growth plans because it has already secured the land and received the necessary regulatory approval.

REASONS TO BE BEARISH
► BioFuel is a development-stage company, and until its two facilities in Nebraska and Minnesota begin producing ethanol it will lose money.
► For the period between April 2006 and December 2006, the company reported a loss of $2.3 million.
► Nothing in the company's literature suggests that it is developing any proprietary technology that will help it remain competitive with advances in cellulosic ethanol such as POET and Iogen are pursuing.

continued

BioFuel Energy continued

WHAT TO WATCH FOR   Execution is the name of the game for BioFuel. Investors are encouraged to monitor the company's progress in getting all five of its ethanol plants up and operational as soon as possible.

CONCLUSION   Neutral. BioFuel's relationship with Cargill suggests that after the ethanol industry shakeout it could be one of the handful of companies that survive. However, unless it is more open about how it intends to improvement the efficiency of its ethanol production, investors should remain skeptical of its ability to deliver profits.

Biofuel Companies

BFRE	COMPANY	BlueFire Ethanol
	SYMBOL	BFRE
	TRADING MARKET	Over-the-counter (Pink Sheets)
	ADDRESS	31 Musick Irvine, CA 92618
	PHONE	949-588-3767
	CEO	Arnold R. Klann
	WEB	*www.bluefireethanol.com*

DESCRIPTION   BlueFire Ethanol is a development-stage company seeking to convert cellulosic waste materials, agricultural residues, wood residues, and other biomass crops into ethanol through a proprietary process. The company's long-term plan is to build biorefinery facilities on or near landfills, waste collection, and waste separations sites in order to reduce landfill costs and better serve urban markets.

REASONS TO BE BULLISH

▶ In 2007, BlueFire was just one of six cellulosic ethanol companies to receive a large grant ($40 million) from the U.S. Department of Energy to develop a solid waste biorefinery facility in Southern California.

▶ The company has been testing its technology for more than five years, and initial testing has now been completed. Company officials claim the tests have been a success (although there has no independent verification of this claim).

▶ If its technology is successful, the company will have found a unique niche by utilizing landfill waste. In addition to helping municipalities across the country lower their operational costs, the technology could be even more environmentally friendly because it is reported to capture methane gas (which is an even more potent greenhouse gas than carbon dioxide).

▶ Unlike other ethanol companies that are overly dependent on corn, BlueFire has no such issues.

continued

BlueFire Ethanol continued

REASONS TO BE BEARISH

► To date, BlueFire's demonstration pilot plant is very small, and the technology has not been fully borne out. A full plant is not expected to be operational until 2009.

► The company is overly reliant on government grants at this time. It is not clear that its technology can successfully compete with either ethanol or other cellulosic-related technologies in the absence of government support.

WHAT TO WATCH FOR   BlueFire's success hinges on its ability to produce cellulosic ethanol at a competitive cost. Investors are urged to watch for information that addresses this issue. As a benchmark, the Department of Energy is estimating that the production of cellulosic ethanol will be $1.07 per gallon by 2012. Investors are also reminded to watch for the development of additional biorefineries. The creation of even a second facility will be a positive sign.

CONCLUSION   Bearish. BlueFire Ethanol has an intriguing technology, and it is pursuing a unique niche. If it is successful, the company could do extremely well. At the current time, though, its technology is too immature, and there are a number of competitors—such as Iogen, Mascoma, Abengoa, and Range Fuels—operating in the same space that bear watching.

Biofuel Companies

COMPANY	Cilion, Inc.
INVESTORS	Khosla Partners, Virgin Fuels, Yucaipa Companies, and Advanced Equities
ADDRESS	31120 West Street Goshen, CA 93227
PHONE	559-302-2500
CEO	Jeremy Wilhelm
WEB	*www.cilion.com*

DESCRIPTION Formed in 2006 through a partnership with Khosla Partners, Western Milling, and Praj Industries, Cilion raised a staggering $235 million in the second half of 2006 and plans to build eight ethanol plants—each capable of producing 55 million gallons annually. The bulk of its plants will be located in California.

WHY IT IS DISRUPTIVE At the present, Cilion is a straight-up ethanol company seeking to produce ethanol more efficiently than its competitors. Because of its relationship with Western Milling, which has expertise in ethanol production, grain handling, logistics, and feed, it is well positioned to achieve this goal. Furthermore, its relationship with Praj Industries (which specializes in building ethanol plants) suggests that it should be able to build its eight plants in a more cost-effective manner than its competitors. Finally, the fact that Cilion will primarily serve the California market implies that it will not need to assume large transportation costs in order to get its product to this lucrative market.

WHAT TO WATCH FOR The company has indicated that it will have all eight plants operational by 2008. If Cilion can achieve this goal of producing 440 million gallons annually, it will be among the larger ethanol producers in the country. Because the company is heavily supported by Vinod Khosla, whose venture capital firm has also invested in a number of cellulosic ethanol companies such as Mascoma and Range Fuels, it is possible that Cilion will more easily be able to make the transition to cellulosic ethanol in the event that that technology comes to fruition. Potential investors are encouraged to monitor whether the company makes good on its ability to efficiently produce enough ethanol so that it can compete with the cost of gasoline even if the price of oil drops back down to $50 a barrel.

continued

CONCLUSION   Bullish. On scale alone, Cilion will be a formidable ethanol producer. The fact that the state of California has mandated that 20 percent of all its biofuel is to come from within the state by 2010 (in 2007 less than 10 percent did) and 40 percent by 2020, suggests that the company will have a large and growing market into which it can supply its ethanol for the foreseeable future. Longer term, its ability to make the transition to cellulosic ethanol works in its favor.

DIL	COMPANY	Dyadic International, Inc.
	SYMBOL	DIL
	TRADING MARKET	AMEX
	ADDRESS	140 Intracoastal Pointe Drive, Suite 404 Jupiter, FL 33477
	PHONE	561-743-8333
	CEO	Mark Emalfarb
	WEB	*www.dyadic.com*

DESCRIPTION   Dyadic International is a biotechnology company conducting research and development activities for the discovery, development, and manufacture of products for the bioenergy, industrial enzyme, and pharmaceutical industries. Recently, the company has been dedicating an increasing portion of its business to developing enzymes for producing fermentable sugars from agricultural feedstocks that could be used for manufacturing cellulosic ethanol.

REASONS TO BE BULLISH

► In 2006, Dyadic entered into a nonexclusive research and development and commercialization agreement with Abengoa Bioenergy for the production of cellulosic ethanol. As part of the deal, Abengoa paid Dyadic $10 million in return for 2.1 million shares of its stock. The deal can be seen as a partial validation of Dyadic's technology.

► In 2007, the company joined Royal Nedalco, one of Europe's leading bioethanol producers, in a project to develop technologies to produce ethanol from sugar beet pulp and wheat bran.

► According to company officials, Dyadic continues to make progress in developing new enzyme mixtures that are converting biomass feedstocks into higher yields.

REASONS TO BE BEARISH

► In mid-2007, the company's CEO Mark Emalfarb was placed on a leave of absence as a result of possible financial improprieties at the company's Chinese operations. An independent audit determined that prior financial reports were not credible. As a result, the American Stock Exchange halted the trading of its stock.

continued

► Even with the unofficial, unaudited numbers, the company still lost $10.9 million for the year. It is quite possible that the revised numbers will be even worse.

► In spite of its emphasis on bioenergy, the company continues to derive the bulk of its revenue from selling enzymes to the textile and paper and pulp industries. Thus it is not accurate to characterize Dyadic as a pure cleantech company.

► While it may be true that Dyadic is having some success at creating new enzyme mixtures that yield a higher conversion rate, it is clear that the rates have not yet reached a level that is commercially viable.

► Dyadic faces a great deal of competition in the field of developing an innovative process for producing cellulosic ethanol. Competitors include Iogen, Mascoma, Verenium, Cilion, and others.

WHAT TO WATCH FOR   The first and most obvious thing to watch for is news relating to the true financial situation of the company. Until this issue is resolved, a dark cloud will continue to linger over Dyadic and its future prospects. Beyond that, investors are strongly encouraged to watch for progress that it has successfully developed enzymes for Abengoa Bioenergy. If it begins to receive sizable royalty payments from the company, that will be a bullish sign.

CONCLUSION   Bearish. The possibility of financial improprieties along with an untested technology that is facing a great deal of competition makes Dyadic far too risky to recommend. Investors are encouraged to focus on alternative investments.

COMPANY	E3 BioFuels
INVESTORS	Private (not publicly available)
ADDRESS	5425 Martindale, Suite 100 Shawnee, KS 66218
PHONE	913-441-1800
CEO	Dennis Langley
WEB	*www.e3biofuels.com*

DESCRIPTION   E3 BioFuels is a privately funded ethanol producer and one of the first companies to employ a closed-loop system for the production of ethanol. Its first 25-million-gallon-a-year facility went into production in the summer of 2007.

WHY IT IS DISRUPTIVE   Most ethanol plants are powered by natural gas or coal. E3 BioFuels is instead placing cow manure into large anaerobic digesters and then having microbes efficiently convert the waste into biogas. This biogas, in turn, is used to power the boilers in the ethanol plant instead of natural gas. This is significant because it has the potential to fundamentally transform the net-energy impact of the ethanol produced. Using natural gas, it has been estimated that one gallon of fossil fuel is needed to produce between 1.3 and 1.8 gallons of ethanol. Using methane, however, the ratio increases to 4 or 5 gallons of ethanol per gallon of fossil fuel. The system has other advantages as well. For instance, because it uses massive amounts of cow manure—which is a leading producer of methane and is a major greenhouse gas contributor—it holds the potential to have a positive impact on climate change. Furthermore, the silage that is left over from the anaerobic process can be used as fertilizer and the wet distiller grain (the stuff left over after ethanol is produced) can be fed directly to cattle. The combination of these advantages makes E3's process an almost closed-loop system. One final benefit of the company's process is that because it uses so much manure it might also help keep groundwater supplies from being contaminated by large feedlots.

continued

E3 BioFuels continued

WHAT TO WATCH FOR   E3 BioFuels' system became operational in July 2007. At this time, it is too early to assess whether the technology and its systems are working as planned. The company has indicated that it wants to build three additional plants for the next five years. If the company's technology works as promised and if it can scale to these levels, the fact that it won't have to use any natural gas to produce ethanol will provide it with a huge economic advantage over other ethanol producers.

CONCLUSION   Bullish. Although the company is privately owned at this time, if it can scale up to over 100 million gallons annually (which should not be a problem provided its technology works as promised) and if it goes public, investors are encouraged to give the company a serious look. Before doing so, though, it is worth considering that Panda Ethanol is producing a comparable technology. It is also possible that scientists at larger companies such as ADM and Cargill are also aggressively producing similar technology.

> **Biofuel Companies**

COMPANY	EcoSynthetix
INVESTORS	Cargill Ventures, H.B. Fuller Ventures, VentureLink Diversified Balanced Fund, and 401 Capital Partners
ADDRESS	3900 Collins Road Lansing, MI 48910
PHONE	517-336-4623
CEO	John van Leeuwen
WEB	*www.ecosynthetix.com*

DESCRIPTION EcoSynthetix is a clean technology company seeking to replace a variety of petroleum-based industrial products, such as polyvinyl acetate and polyvinyl alcohol, with nanobiomaterials.

WHY IT IS DISRUPTIVE EcoSynthetix has developed a proprietary process for radically reducing the size of natural cornstarch. When reduced to the nanoscale, the nanoparticles have 400 times more surface area than natural starch granules. This means they require less water when used to produce adhesive; and this, in turn, means that less energy and time is required to dry the coatings. For an average size plastic plant this could result in natural gas savings of almost $1 million a year. As an added benefit, because the nanoparticles are derived from corn and not petroleum, the resultant plastic is biodegradable.

WHAT TO WATCH FOR In 2006, it was reported that a supplier of the "clamshell" boxes to McDonald's was incorporating EcoSynthetix technology. If additional large suppliers begin utilizing the technology, that will be a bullish sign.

CONCLUSION Neutral. While EcoSynthetix technology appears to deliver the stated benefits, it faces competition from companies such as NatureWorks LLC and Metabolix. Should the company go public, investors will want to conduct a side-by-side analysis of its technology with these other companies and discern which has lined up the most corporate customers.

Biofuel Companies

COMPANY	GreenFuel Technologies Corporation
INVESTORS	Polaris Venture Partners, Access Industries, and Draper Fisher Jurvetson
ADDRESS	735 Concord Avenue Cambridge, MA 02138
PHONE	617-234-0077
CEO	Bob Metcalfe
WEB	*www.greenfuelonline.com*

DESCRIPTION   GreenFuel Technologies is an early-development-stage company attempting to pioneer the development of an algae bioreactor technology, dubbed Emissions-to-Biofuels. The technology seeks to efficiently convert carbon dioxide from the smokestack gases of coal-fired power plants and other carbon-dioxide-producing facilities into clean, renewable biofuels.

WHY IT IS DISRUPTIVE   Algae are unicellular plants, and like all plants they divide and grow using photosynthesis. According to GreenFuel, its proprietary process can absorb a significant percentage (perhaps up to 40 percent) of a power plant's carbon dioxide emissions every day. The technology, which is being actively explored by leading power companies such as NRG Energy, has a surprising number of potential benefits. For starters, it can significantly reduce carbon dioxide emissions without requiring energy companies to undergo an extensive retooling or modification. Thus it has the potential to earn companies valuable emission credits and government tax subsidies, while also improving a company's image as a clean manufacturer. Furthermore, because the algae can be converted into any number of different biofuels, including ethanol, biodiesel, methane, and solid biomass, it can be used as an energy source. In this way, it could either help a coal company create revenue from biofuel sales or reduce its exposure to fossil price volatility.

continued

WHAT TO WATCH FOR   GreenFuel remains a development-stage company and it is not clear at this time whether its technology can scale to industrial capacity levels or if it can compete favorably with other carbon-dioxide-reducing technologies, such as carbon sequestration or nanoparticle catalysts. GreenFuel's first big test will be the pilot project the company is conducting with NRG Energy at a 1,500 MW coal plant in Louisiana. If that project receives good reviews, it will be a positive sign that the technology might soon be used to begin retrofitting the country's large fleet of carbon-dioxide-emitting coal-fired power plants. Interested parties should also watch for similar news from a test the company is conducting with Global Renewable Energy Efficiency Network (GREEN), a new biofuels company in South Africa, as well as any news that the company's relationship with İGV, a large private industrial research institute in Germany, is bearing fruit.

CONCLUSION   Bearish. GreenFuel has a strong management team and board of directors, but after a failed bioreactor test in the summer of 2007 the company was forced to lay off half of its workforce. Moving forward, this failure could make it difficult for the company to raise additional money. If, however, the company's technology can "eat" carbon dioxide as promised and then effectively and efficiently convert it into a biofuel by 2009, there is reason to believe that it could become a valuable tool for coal companies looking to reduce their carbon footprint. The company is privately owned at this time and should remain that way for some time. In the event GreenFuel needs to look to the public market for financing, investors would be advised to stay away—its technology is simply too unproven at this time.

COMPANY	Imperium Renewables
INVESTORS	Nth Power, Ardsley Partners, Technology Partners, BlackRock, Inc., Silver Point Capital, Treaty Oak Capital, and others
ADDRESS	1418 Third Avenue, Suite 300 Seattle, WA 98101
PHONE	206-254-0204
CEO	Martin Tobias
WEB	*www.imperiumrenewables.com*

DESCRIPTION   Founded as Seattle Biodiesel, LLC in 2003, Imperium Renewables is seeking to become a national leader in next-generation biodiesel refining and manufacturing technology. In 2007, the company raised over $100 million in venture capital and an additional $120 million debt financing to begin building a facility in Washington state capable of producing 100 million gallons of biodiesel annually. In May 2007, the company filed papers to go public but at the time of publication the deal was still pending.

WHY IT IS DISRUPTIVE   The company's goal is to utilize proprietary technology, including its ultra-efficient Pressurized "Pulse Reactor," its Active Methanol Recovery System, and its Adsorbent Enhanced Polishing Process, to deliver a gallon of biodiesel cheaper than a petroleum facility can manufacture diesel fuel. Because Imperium's biodiesel is manufactured from vegetable oil, including soybeans, canola, and palm oil, it is 100 percent renewable, and as an added benefit, it emits 78 percent less carbon dioxide. Other advantages the company has going for it include its present status as the only large-scale biodiesel facility in the western United States and its having had its biodiesel approved to ASTM standards, meaning that it performs just as well as, if not better than, regular diesel fuel.

continued

WHAT TO WATCH FOR   Imperium has publicly stated that it intends to be producing 400 million gallons annually by the end of 2008, with large-scale facilities in Washington, Hawaii, Argentina, and the Northeastern United States. If it can achieve this ambitious goal, it will be among the largest biodiesel producers in the nation. However, in order to achieve this goal, the company will likely need to raise additional capital, and it will be dependent upon the continued subsidization of biodiesel by the federal government.

CONCLUSION   Bullish. Although Imperium will face competition in the United States from ADM and SE Energy and abroad from companies such as Brenco in Brazil, Ensus in the United Kingdom, and China Agri-Industries Holdings in China, the global economy's growing demand for cleaner-burning biodiesel is likely to utilize all of the biodiesel that is produced. As the only large supplier of biodiesel in the western United States and Canada, the company should also enjoy a competitive advantage in the area of the world where the demand for its product will likely be the highest. If there is a danger, it is that Imperium will need to broaden its supply of vegetable oils beyond soybeans from the Midwest and palm oil from Malaysia. The best-case scenario is for Imperium to get farmers in Washington State to supply it with more canola oil. In the event Imperium goes public, investors looking for a slightly higher risk/high reward investment are encouraged to consider the company. If it can achieve its goal of 400 million gallons by the end of 2008, it should be able to leverage the revenue from that growth to support additional growth across the globe.

Biofuel Companies

COMPANY	Iogen Corporation
INVESTORS	Goldman Sachs, Royal Dutch Shell, Petro-Canada
ADDRESS	310 Hunt Club Road East Ottawa, Ontario, Canada K1V 1C1
PHONE	613-733-9830
CEO	Brian Foody
WEB	*www.iogen.ca*

DESCRIPTION   Iogen is a biotechnology company specializing in cellulosic ethanol made from farm waste. The company has developed and patented enzymes that can extract sugars from wheat and barley straw. The company is also developing enzymes that can be used to modify and improve the processing of natural fibers in the textile, animal feed, and paper and pulp industries. The company currently has a pilot facility operational in Canada; in 2007 it received a large grant (up to $80 million) from the U.S. Department of Energy to build a second plant in Idaho, which will be able to produce 18 million gallons of ethanol annually from wheat straw, barley straw, corn stover, and switchgrass.

WHY IT IS DISRUPTIVE   Currently, Iogen's enzymes can produce ethanol from various feedstocks for around $1.35 a gallon. This is not yet competitive with existing ethanol production techniques, but if the company can continue to refine its process and production capability, or can find and patent new enzymes, its cellulosic ethanol could become competitive with other technologies in the near future. Furthermore, the fact that the company already has an operational facility gives it a leg up on other competitors such as Range Fuels and Verenium.

continued

WHAT TO WATCH FOR   The company's long-term plan is to license its enzymes to other ethanol producers. This is a fairly unique business model and it could serve the company very well. Investors are encouraged to watch for news that other ethanol companies are, in fact, licensing its technology. Investors are further advised to monitor the status of the company's facility in Idaho. It is expected to begin producing ethanol by 2009. Longer term, if Range Fuels' technology is successful, it could make the use of enzymes less important in the future. Therefore, investors must monitor the status of competing technologies.

CONCLUSION   Bullish. The fact that the company already has an operational facility is a positive sign, as is its existing relationship with Royal Dutch Shell. Furthermore, in addition to playing in the ethanol field, Iogen is more diversified than many other ethanol companies in that its enzyme technology can also be used in the animal feed and paper industries. Should the company go public, investors are encouraged to give it a strong look.

COMPANY	Mascoma
INVESTORS	Khosla Ventures, General Catalyst Partners, Flagship Ventures, Kleiner Perkins Caufield & Byers, VantagePoint Venture Partners, Atlas Venture, and Pinnacle Ventures
ADDRESS	161 First Street, Second Floor East Cambridge, MA 02142
PHONE	717-234-0099
CEO	Bruce Jamerson
WEB	*www.mascoma.com*

DESCRIPTION   Mascoma is an early-stage cellulosic biomass-to-ethanol company.

WHY IT IS DISRUPTIVE   Unlike Synthetic Genomics' approach to creating cellulosic ethanol by manufacturing a synthetic cell from scratch, Mascoma is seeking to modify an existing microbe by adding desired genetic pathways from other organisms and disabling undesirable characteristics. Depending on the microbe involved, the company will follow one of two procedures. An organism that naturally metabolizes cellulose can be modified to produce higher yields of ethanol from wood, straw, switchgrass, and other biomass; alternatively, bacteria whose only fermentation product is ethanol can be engineered to live in high-temperature environments. If successful, Mascoma has the potential to produce cellulosic ethanol at a very low cost from abundant feedstocks which are readily available in most parts of the United States. In 2006, the company raised over $30 million to begin construction of a modest-sized pilot project in New York state. As part of the deal the company also received $15 million in grants from the state. In 2007, Mascoma was one of six companies to receive funding ($5 million) from the federal government to pursue cellulosic research. It also named former U.S. Senate Majority Leader Tom Daschle to its board of directors.

continued

WHAT TO WATCH FOR Mascoma has already established key partnerships with a number of other companies. It has an ongoing relationship with Genencor—a division of the Danish conglomerate Danisco—to produce enzymes that might efficiently break down lignocellulosic ethanol; and it has licensed yeast-based cellulosic technology from Royal Nedalco, a leading European ethanol technology company. Perhaps more significantly, it is also working with Tamarack Energy to collaborate on the building of the New York facility and, possibly, additional facilities throughout the Northeast United States.

CONCLUSION Neutral. Until Mascoma's New York pilot project is up and operational, it is difficult to assess the effectiveness of its technology. In general, however, cellulosic ethanol, while still a few years removed from becoming a mainstream technology, appears to have the potential to produce ethanol at a lower cost than corn-based ethanol and thus warrants investor attention. Nevertheless, Mascoma is one of just a handful of promising companies pursuing cellulosic ethanol. In the event the company goes public, before considering an investment in Mascoma investors are strongly encouraged to first review and compare the status of the following companies' cellulosic ethanol technology: Abengoa, Iogen, BlueFire Ethanol, POET, and Range Fuels.

Biofuel Companies

MBLX	COMPANY	Metabolix, Inc.
	SYMBOL	MBLX
	TRADING MARKET	NASDAQ
	ADDRESS	21 Erie Street Cambridge, MA 02139
	PHONE	617-492-0505
	CEO	Jay Kouba
	WEB	*www.metabolix.com*

DESCRIPTION   Metabolix is a biotechnology company dedicated to the development of alternatives to petrochemical-based plastics, fuels, and chemicals. Applying the tools of molecular biology, it has produced natural plastics that are biodegradable and have potential applications in everything from packaging and consumer goods to medical implants.

REASONS TO BE BULLISH

► In 2006, Metabolix formed Telles, a fifty-fifty joint venture with ADM, to commercialize the production of Mirel, a natural plastic. By 2008, the plant is expected to produce 100 million pounds of natural plastic annually.

► Mirel can be used as an alternative to petroleum-based plastics in a wide variety of conversion processes, including injection molding, paper coating, and thermoforming. It can even be used as a material in medical implants and tissue engineering.

► The fact that Mirel is biodegradable will likely appeal to environmentally conscious consumers as well as large corporations looking to improve their environmental image. If more cities and states follow San Francisco's lead and prohibit the use of nonbiodegradable plastics, Metabolix could be a prime beneficiary.

► Metabolix's plastic biodegrades without industrial composting or incineration.

REASONS TO BE BEARISH

► At the time of publication, Metabolix was trading much higher than its original IPO price of $14. This is in spite of the fact that it is not yet generating much in the way of revenue.

continued

► The plastics industry, which historically has very low margins, is not likely to embrace natural plastics until it is convinced that natural plastics will be competitive in terms of costs and will perform to the specifications that its customers have come to expect.

► Metabolix will face competition from NatureWorks LLC as well as larger plastics companies such as DuPont and BASF.

WHAT TO WATCH FOR   If the Telles plant becomes operational in 2008 and Metabolix finds a market for all 100 million pounds of its natural plastic, investors can take that as a bullish indicator that the technology and product is meeting with widespread acceptance. Investors will also want to watch for signs that leading consumer companies such as Procter & Gamble or McDonald's are requesting its plastic. Longer term, if Metabolix can move into the medical market, that would be a positive sign; and would suggest that the company might be able to achieve higher margins on more specialized products.

CONCLUSION   Bullish. The stock is currently trading at a high price and investors will want to make sure that the Mirel plant becomes operational in 2008. And even then, it could be a year or two before Metabolix sees any revenue from the deal. This is because ADM made the up-front investment in the manufacturing facility and will receive the bulk of those revenues until its investment has been paid off. Nevertheless, over 350 billion pounds of plastics is consumed every year in America (and accounts for nearly 10 percent of total U.S. oil consumption). If Metabolix can capture even a portion of this market, it could become a very profitable business.

Biofuel Companies

COMPANY	NatureWorks LLC
INVESTORS	Cargill
ADDRESS	15305 Minnetonka Boulevard Minnetonka, MN 55435
PHONE	877-423-7659
CEO	Dennis McGrew
WEB	*www.nautreworksllc.com*

DESCRIPTION   NatureWorks is wholly owned by Cargill. The company applies its proprietary technology to the processing of natural plant sugars to create a biodegradable and environmentally friendly polylactide acid, which is marketed under the brand of NatureWorks. The bio-friendly plastic is currently being used in a variety of commercial products throughout Europe and in the United States, including in Green Mountain Coffee cups and Mrs. Fields Cookies packaging.

WHY IT IS DISRUPTIVE   Because the plastics are derived from plants, it has been estimated that NatureWorks' production process uses 68 percent less fossil fuel resources than traditional plastics. The company's plastic has also been certified as the first greenhouse-gas-neutral polymer on the market.

WHAT TO WATCH FOR   Being greenhouse-gas-neutral, NatureWorks would benefit from the imposition of any regulations limiting greenhouse gas emissions. Another factor that is likely to contribute to its growth is the development of improved polymers that can be used for a number of different applications. Among those currently under development are natural plastics suitable for clothing as well as more durable plastics necessary for thermoplastic applications.

CONCLUSION   It has been estimated that biopolymers could reduce by 94 percent the amount of plastic consumer products that end up in local disposal facilities. And while it will likely be some time before such a goal is achieved, it speaks to the potential of NatureWorks technology. At this time, it is unlikely that Cargill would allow the company to go public, but in the event that it does, investors are encouraged to consider an investment.

Biofuel Companies

PEIX		
	COMPANY	Pacific Ethanol
	SYMBOL	PEIX
	TRADING MARKET	NASDAQ
	ADDRESS	400 Capitol Mall, Suite 2060 Sacramento, CA 95814
	PHONE	916-403-2123
	CEO	Neil Koehler
	WEB	*www.pacificethanol.net*

DESCRIPTION   Pacific Ethanol is currently the largest West Coast–based marketer and producer of ethanol, and its stated goal is to produce 420 million gallons of ethanol annually by 2010 to meet California's and the surrounding region's growing demand for ethanol.

REASONS TO BE BULLISH

► Annual revenues are increasing and jumped from $87.6 million in 2005 to $226 million in 2006. Equally significant, net losses decreased over the same period from $5 million to $3 million.

► The state of California already consumes close to 1 billion gallons of ethanol and, as the company closest to this large market (the state represents about 25 percent of total United States consumption), Pacific Ethanol is well positioned to profit from this proximity.

► The company appears to be well positioned to meet its goal of having five production facilities operational on the West Coast by 2008. In early 2007, it announced plans to begin construction on two 50-million-gallon facilities. One in Stockton (near San Francisco) and the other in Calipatria will serve the Southern California market.

► In 2006, Bill Gates's money management firm, Cascade Investment, acquired a 25 percent stake in the company.

continued

REASONS TO BE BEARISH

► The company is still not profitable and its rapid expansion could delay profitability.

► Pacific Ethanol's strategy for hedging against higher corn prices is unknown. To the extent that competitors such as ADM or Aventine Renewable Energy do a better job at securing long-term corn contracts at lower prices, the company could find itself at a competitive disadvantage in the future if corn prices continue to increase.

► The company does not have a well-articulated strategy for moving into the cellulosic ethanol market.

► It will face additional competition once Cilion has its three 55-million-gallon facilities operational in California by the end of 2007.

► In mid-2007, senior executives began unloading a significant number of shares at a price of $15 a share.

WHAT TO WATCH FOR   Investors should keep a close eye on whether Pacific Ethanol meets its goal of producing 420 million gallons of ethanol by 2010. If it does, the company should be able to increase revenues, lower costs, and become profitable.

CONCLUSION   Neutral. By focusing on a narrow but large niche market (the Western United States), Pacific Ethanol is well positioned for growth. The fact that its facilities will be close to the markets it seeks to serve should allow the company to maintain a price advantage on competitors by keeping transportation costs low. However, Pacific Ethanol will need to run a very tight ship in order to compete with newer competitors such as Cilion and Panda Ethanol. Longer term, the outlook for the company becomes a bit hazier because in order to stay competitive with ethanol exports from Brazil, it will need to continue to lower costs. Also, unless Pacific Ethanol has plans to expand into the cellulosic ethanol and biodiesel markets, it could find itself controlling an ever-smaller part of the alternative fuel market.

Biofuel Companies

PDAE	COMPANY	Panda Ethanol
	SYMBOL	PDAE
	TRADING MARKET	Over-the-counter
	ADDRESS	4100 Spring Valley, Suite 100 Dallas, TX 75244
	PHONE	972-361-1200
	CEO	Todd Carter
	WEB	*www.pandaethanol.com*

DESCRIPTION   Panda Ethanol is currently developing six 105-million-gallon-per-year ethanol facilities located in Texas, Colorado, Kansas, and Nebraska. The facilities are categorized as "denatured" projects because, unlike most ethanol plants, which are powered by natural gas, Panda's facilities will be powered by cattle manure. The company's founder is Panda Energy International, a privately held energy company generating in excess of 9,000 MW of electric generation.

REASONS TO BE BULLISH

► Critics have long complained that traditional ethanol production typically consumes almost as much fossil fuel as it saves. By utilizing manure, which it receives free of charge from cattle farmers from the surrounding areas (who are only too happy to be unburdened of the waste), Panda can dramatically lower its energy costs and, thus, its cost to produce ethanol.

► Because Panda's process doesn't utilize natural gas, it also avoids exposure to the volatile nature of the cost of that energy source.

► As an added benefit, because the process prevents the release of methane (which is a powerful greenhouse gas), Panda could be in a position to benefit from any regulatory schemes that seek to limit or restrict greenhouse gases.

► Panda is often able to strike favorable financing deals with local authorities who are not only pleased to have a large ethanol facility located in their town but are also anxious to eliminate some of the nasty problems that often accompany the large feedlots.

continued

- ► Because the company always locates itself in proximity to large herds of cattle, it also has a ready market for ethanol's waste product—distiller's grain, which can be used as feed for cattle.
- ► With facilities in Texas, Colorado, Kansas, and Nebraska, it is closer to the California market than many other ethanol producers.

REASONS TO BE BEARISH
- ► Each manure-powered ethanol facility costs up to $40 million more to build than a natural gas power ethanol plant because the process is more complex and capital intensive. If the price natural gas drops, it could be hard hit.

WHAT TO WATCH FOR   Panda's first facility in Hereford, Texas, is expected to be operational by 2008. It has also begun construction of the facility in Yuma, Colorado. Investors will want to make sure that both facilities are operating smoothly before investing.

CONCLUSION   Bullish. Although Panda is traded as an over-the-counter stock and is thus not subject to all the reporting requirements of companies traded on the New York Stock Exchange and NASDAQ, its unique business model warrants strong consideration as a possible investment. The fact that its process helps solve a problem for farmers and communities (by removing manure), is environmentally friendly (because it reduces the amount of methane released into the atmosphere), and can lower the price of ethanol production by eliminating the costs normally associated with natural gas makes it a classic win-win-win situation. Longer term, if Panda can fulfill its goal of bringing six 105-million-gallon ethanol facilities online, it could be one of the largest ethanol producers in the country.

Biofuel Companies

COMPANY	POET Energy (formerly Broin Companies)
INVESTORS	Private (not publicly available)
ADDRESS	4615 Lewis Avenue Sioux Falls, SD 57104
PHONE	605-965-2200
CEO	Jeff Broin
WEB	*www.poetenergy.com*

DESCRIPTION POET Energy is the largest dry mill ethanol producer in the United States; it currently manages twenty plants in five states and has another six plants under development. The company has been in the ethanol business for more than twenty years and is highly specialized in the technological development, production, and marketing of ethanol. As of 2007, it was producing over 1 billion gallons of ethanol annually.

WHY IT IS DISRUPTIVE In addition to its size, POET is developing two different breakthrough technologies that are expected to help the company produce more ethanol with significantly less energy per bushel of corn. The first is its BPX technology, a patent-pending raw-starch hydrolysis process that converts starch into sugar and then ferments without using any heat. This process not only reduces energy costs but, because it also increases the protein content of ethanol coproducts (primarily animal feed), it can also help increase the company's profit margins.

The second technology is dubbed BFrac, and it separates the corn into three fractions: fiber, germ, and endosperm. The endosperm is converted into ethanol, and the other components are turned into higher-yield coproducts.

The real reason POET represents a disruptive threat, however, centers on the company's relationship with DuPont. In late 2006, the two companies agreed to develop a technology package that can efficiently break down the complex sugar matrix found in corn stover and transform it into ethanol. The process appears to represent a real transition in the production of cellulosic ethanol, and the 125-million-gallon plant it is developing is expected to be operational by 2010. If it works as promised, it could allow POET to gain a significant competitive advantage over those other companies that are just producing corn ethanol. To help aid the project, POET has received a grant of up to $80 million from the U.S. Department of Energy.

continued

WHAT TO WATCH FOR   The project with DuPont is known as Project LIBERTY (Launch of an Integrated Bio-refinery with Eco-sustainable and Renewable Technologies in Y2009). Company officials claim that it will be able to produce 11 percent more etha-. nol from a bushel of corn, while using 83 percent less energy. If it can deliver on this promise, POET should remain one of the largest and most successful ethanol companies in America.

CONCLUSION   Bullish. Although POET is a privately owned company and is thus not available to individual investors at this time, it is the type of company investors need to keep their eye on. It is likely to be one of the few ethanol companies that will still be standing after the industry reaches maturity and many of the smaller companies have either gone out of business or been acquired by the more successful companies. In the event it does go public, investors are encouraged to revisit the status of Project LIBERTY and, if it is successful, consider an investment.

Biofuel Companies

COMPANY	Range Fuels
INVESTORS	Khosla Ventures
ADDRESS	11101 W. 120th Avenue, Suite 200 Broomfield, CO 80021
PHONE	303-410-2100
CEO	Mitch Mandich
WEB	*www.rangefuels.com*

DESCRIPTION   Range Fuels is a privately held company employing a proprietary thermochemical process, termed K2, to convert biomass to a synthetic gas and then into ethanol. In 2007, the company received a sizable $76 million grant from the U.S. Department of Energy to help build its first production facility.

WHY IT IS DISRUPTIVE   Range Fuels' technology is disruptive for a couple of reasons. First, like other cellulosic ethanol companies, it holds the potential of being able to use agricultural products other than corn to manufacture ethanol. These include wood, switchgrass, and miscanthus grass. Second, Range Fuels claims its system eliminates the use of enzymes in the production of ethanol, and enzymes are an expensive component of traditional cellulosic ethanol production. Third, because the company makes cellulosic ethanol through anaerobic thermal conversion rather than fermentation or acid hydrolysis, the process converts the feedstock into ethanol at a significantly faster rate. Finally, Range Fuels has developed a modular system that allows the company to place facilities near feedstocks (such as municipal waste sites or forest plants) as well as scale up production capacity on a fast basis.

WHAT TO WATCH FOR   The company's lead funder believes that in the longterm (ten years), Range Fuels' technology can drive the price of ethanol production down to $1.00 a gallon. In the meantime, interested parties should watch to ensure that the company meets its short-term goal of building a 40-million-gallon facility in Georgia by 2008–2009. Mid-term, the establishment of additional production facilities in close proximity to various feedstocks will be a bullish sign that the company is moving in

continued

the right direction of meeting its other goal of producing 1 billion gallons of ethanol annually. There is also some concern that Range Fuel's ethanol might have a lower net energy balance than other cellulosic ethanol methods. (At this time, this claim is difficult to assess but would-be investors are advised to stay atop of this issue.)

CONCLUSION   Bullish. The company is well funded and has an experienced management team and a strong scientific advisory team. Provided Range Fuels' unique thermal conversion process works and can deliver the cost advantages that company officials suggest, investors are encouraged to consider an investment in the event the company goes public.

Biofuel Companies

COMPANY	Solazyme, Inc.
INVESTORS	Roda Group, Harris & Harris Group, and individual investors
ADDRESS	571 Eccles Avenue South San Francisco, CA 94080
PHONE	650-780-4777
CEO	Harrison F. Dillon
WEB	*www.solazyme.com*

DESCRIPTION Solazyme is an early-development-stage company conducting research to synthetically evolve algae to produce a variety of valuable pharmaceutical, nutraceutical, and bioindustrial products using genetic engineering methods.

WHY IT IS DISRUPTIVE Because photosynthetic microbes require nothing more than sunlight, water, and inexpensive trace minerals—and hence have low cost and high ease of use—they are preferable for the production of high-value molecules. As an added benefit, the process does not require a large investment in manufacturing infrastructure. In 2006, Solazyme received a grant from the federal government to pursue the development of a particular type of algae that might be able to produce biodiesel.

WHAT TO WATCH FOR Solazyme is also working on algae that can produce high-value molecules that have utility in the nutraceutical and cosmetic industries. If Solazyme can successfully produce these products, it might provide the company the necessary capital to expand into the biofuel arena.

CONCLUSION Bearish. Until the company creates a successful commercial product, its technology is nothing more than a promising laboratory project. Investors are not encouraged to get excited about the technology until it attracts the attention of a major energy company or until Solazyme demonstrates that it can produce the algae on a commercial scale. In the event the company does go public, investors are encouraged to review the status of GreenFuel and Synthetic Genomics' technologies, because they could render Solazyme's technology obsolete.

Biofuel Companies

COMPANY	Synthetic Genomics
INVESTORS	Private (not publicly available)
ADDRESS	9601 Blackwell Road Rockville, MD 20850
PHONE	240-238-0800
CEO	Dr. J. Craig Venter
WEB	*www.syntheticgenomics.com*

DESCRIPTION   The company was founded by Craig Venter, one of the world's foremost scientists, who is widely recognized for his valuable contributions to sequencing and analyzing the human genome. Synthetic Genomics seeks to design, synthesize, and assemble specifically engineered cell-level biofactories that allow scientists to make extensive changes to the DNA of a chromosome and then assemble it and insert it into an organism, which will then perform very specific tasks.

WHY IT IS DISRUPTIVE   Essentially what Synthetic Genomics is seeking to create are "designer bacteria." The company begins by determining the minimum set of genes necessary for an organism to survive in a controlled environment, then identifies the desired biological capabilities (which are found by sequencing the DNA of a wide variety of living organisms) and inserts DNA into the host; and the host is then placed into an environment that allows metabolic activity and replication. The 200-plus scientists working on behalf of the company have already developed one synthetic chromosome and are busy designing a proof of concept for two bioenergy applications, hydrogen and ethanol. If the technology works as promised, it could, quite literally, spark a biological industrial revolution—for example, by allowing living organisms to create ethanol by breaking down corn (or any number of other commodities) into a biofuel in one simple step. It is also possible that designer bacteria could be made to do a variety of other things. For instance, it is believed that such organisms might be used for environmental remediation—to clean up polluted land or perhaps even efficiently process carbon dioxide and remove greenhouse gas from the environment.

continued

WHAT TO WATCH FOR   Venter has indicated that his company is in discussions with a number of major energy companies, and in June 2007 it signed a deal with BP to sequence the genes of micro-organisms found in fossil fuel deposits. If Synthetic Genomics signs a similar deal with a company either to produce ethanol or hydrogen or to clean up carbon dioxide (from a coal plant), this will represent a significant validation of its technology. Venter and his team have also been culling an amazing amount of genetic material from the world's oceans. It is possible that some of this new genetic information could be the key to creating highly efficient and effective biofactories.

CONCLUSION   Bullish. The Synthetic Genomics team of scientists has expertise in genomics, microbiology, human and evolutionary biology, bioinformatics, high-throughput DNA sequencing, environmental biology, information technology, biological energy, and synthetic biology. Each of these fields is experiencing near-exponential growth, and to the extent the company can capitalize on this progress it may only be a matter of time before such designer bacteria comes to fruition. Of course, there are still considerable technological risks, and Venter's management style is the subject of some concern, but at present, no other company appears close to achieving the goal of designer bacteria. In the event the company goes public, risk-tolerant investors who can demonstrate some patience are encouraged to consider an investment.

Biofuel Companies

USBE	COMPANY	US BioEnergy Corp.
	SYMBOL	USBE
	TRADING MARKET	NASDAQ
	ADDRESS	5500 Centex Drive Inver Grove Heights, MN 55077
	PHONE	651-355-8300
	CEO	Gordon Ommen
	WEB	*www.usbioenergy.net*

DESCRIPTION   US BioEnergy Corporation produces and markets ethanol and distiller grains. As of September 2007, it had four facilities operational and four more under construction. The majority of the plants are located in the Midwest, and by the end of 2008 the company plans to be producing between 600 and 650 million gallons of ethanol. In additional to selling ethanol, the company also provides facility management and marketing services to third-party ethanol producers. The company went public in December of 2006.

REASONS TO BE BULLISH

► The company turned a slight profit in 2006 and it recorded most of its growth in the fourth quarter.

► With four plants under construction, US BioEnergy is poised for considerable growth.

► With facilities primarily in the Midwest, it is close to the supply of corn and thus has an advantage over companies, such as Pacific Ethanol, that are located on the West Coast.

► US BioEnergy has close to $80 million in cash on hand and should be able to fund additional growth.

► It has established relationships with BP, Marathon Oil, and Valero Energy to market and sell its ethanol.

continued

US BioEnergy Corp. continued

REASONS TO BE BEARISH
▶ Compared to ADM, US BioEnergy is a small player and will face considerable competitive pressure from larger ethanol producers.
▶ Its profits will be closely tied to the price of corn and natural gas.
▶ Unlike other ethanol companies, it does not appear to be investing in cellulosic ethanol and could be vulnerable to the expansion of ethanol produced from something other than corn.

WHAT TO WATCH FOR   US BioEnergy's growth could also be hampered by zoning and permitting issues. Investors should monitor how a lawsuit over a 100-million-gallon facility in Grinnell, Iowa, is resolved. At some point, acquiring ethanol facilities may be more economical than building new ones. If the company begins acquiring smaller ethanol facilities, that will be a sign that it is serious about being one of the larger ethanol producers in the country.

CONCLUSION   Neutral. The company appears well poised to grow through 2008 and its access to markets in the Midwest (where state governments are mandating the use of ethanol) will prove a benefit. However, investors should carefully monitor the company's ability to manage its growth. Longer term, the company will need to address the threat caused by cellulosic ethanol, biobutanol, biodiesel, and other biofuels.

VSE	COMPANY	VeraSun Energy Corporation
	SYMBOL	VSE
	TRADING MARKET	NYSE
	ADDRESS	100 22nd Avenue Brookings, SD 57006
	PHONE	605-696-7200
	CEO	Donald L. Endres
	WEB	*www.verasun.com*

DESCRIPTION VeraSun Energy Corporation engages in the production and sale of ethanol. It is currently producing 600 million gallons of ethanol annually from five facilities in the Midwest. It also has three separate facilities—each capable of producing 110 million gallons annually—under construction. By the end of 2008, VeraSun expects to be producing close to 1 billion gallons of ethanol annually.

REASONS TO BE BULLISH

► The company has, with the exception of one quarter in 2007, been profitable since it was founded in 2001.

► At the present time, it is the third largest ethanol producer in the United States (behind only ADM and POET) and its facilities in Iowa, South Dakota, and southern Minnesota guarantee it a safe supply of corn.

► In 2006, VeraSun announced plans to begin promoting bioethanol E85 with General Motors, and in 2007 it announced deals with Enterprise Rent-a-Cars and Krogers to market its ethanol.

► Also in 2007 the company invested an undisclosed amount of money in a new cellulosic start-up, SunEthanol.

► The company expects to begin producing 110 million gallons of biodiesel annually beginning in 2008.

continued

REASONS TO BE BEARISH

► Since going public in 2006 at $23 a share, VeraSun's stock price is well off its all-time high of $30.

► In 2007, the company suffered a modest loss in the second quarter—primarily as a result of very high corn prices.

► In 2006, VeraSun decided not to renew its contract with Aventine to distribute its products. The transition into the distribution side of the business could cause the company some problems.

► As with all ethanol companies, the race to produce more ethanol could cause ethanol prices to drop.

► In mid-2007, a senior executive sold a sizable number of shares in the neighborhood of $17 a share, fueling speculation that management is not optimistic about the company's near-term prospects.

WHAT TO WATCH FOR   Although VeraSun's move into biodiesel is relatively small, investors are encouraged to keep a close eye on its progress. A number of major automobile manufacturers are planning to introduce biodiesel vehicles by 2009 and that could drive up demand for biodiesel. The company's relationship with General Motors could also prove beneficial if the automobile manufacturer decides to throw its weight behind a major push to get consumers to purchase bioethanol E85.

CONCLUSION   Bullish. The company presently has a forward price-to-earnings ratio of 16. This is in line with the industry. The company's dual strategy of acquiring additional ethanol facilities and investing in cellulosic ethanol is prudent and should position it well for future growth. Furthermore, with over an annual production capacity of 1 billion gallons, VeraSun should be able to achieve the necessary economies of scale to control its margins. The company's expertise in producing ethanol and its ability to manage its transportation costs should also allow it to put a significant amount of competitive pressure on many of the more modest-sized ethanol companies, such as US BioEnergy, Pacific Ethanol, and Aventine. Look for the company to begin acquiring smaller ethanol facilities as the ethanol industry begins to consolidate.

Biofuel Companies

VRNM	COMPANY	Verenium Corporation
	SYMBOL	VRNM
	TRADING MARKET	NASDAQ
	ADDRESS	55 Cambridge Parkway, 8th Floor Cambridge, MA 02142
	PHONE	617-674-5300
	CEO	Carlos A. Rivas
	WEB	*www.celunol.com*

DESCRIPTION In February 2007, Diversa Corporation and Celunol announced that they had signed a definitive merger agreement to create a new cellulosic ethanol company to leverage the two organizations' proprietary technology. The new company was named Verenium. Diversa specializes in the development of high-performance specialty enzymes, which have applications in the alternative fuels, industrial, and health and nutrition markets. Celunol's technology is based on the metabolic engineering of microorganisms to more efficiently produce ethanol from a variety of different feedstocks including rice straw, corn stover, citrus pulp, and sugar cane.

REASONS TO BE BULLISH
- ► Verenium's technology is reported to be able to convert all of the sugar found in cellulosic biomass. This trait should allow the company to manufacture ethanol more economically than corn-based ethanol.
- ► As a result of the merger Verenium has the added benefit of being more diversified than other ethanol companies by supplying enzymes for things other than just the production of ethanol.
- ► To this end, Verenium presently is supplying enzymes to Cargill for the creation of food-related products and to Bunge for the discovery and development of novel enzymes to be used in the production of edible oil products. The company is also conducting joint research and development with Syngenta to develop new enzymes for the production of other biofuels.

continued

REASONS TO BE BEARISH

► Verenium has only two modest-sized pilot projects currently under development: a small 50,000-gallon pilot facility in Louisiana and a larger, 1.4-million-gallon plant in Osaka, Japan. The latter, however, isn't expected to be fully operational until 2009 at the earliest.

► The company is not profitable and might not be until 2011. Because of the cost of acquiring Celunol, it is possible that the company will need to raise more money to finance the building of additional production capacity.

► As of March 2007, the company had $125 million in cash, but at the company's current cash-burn rate that money is expected to last only to the end of 2008.

► The acquisition of Celunol could hurt the sales of enzymes that Diversa was previously making for companies if those customers now view Verenium as a competitor.

WHAT TO WATCH FOR   Verenium's success will rest on its ability to get its two pilot plants producing at full capacity as soon as possible. Investors are encouraged to watch for news that the company will meet its timeline of 2009 for its Osaka plant as well as news that its technology is working as promised at its Louisiana facility.

CONCLUSION   Bearish. The merger has severely hampered the company's financial flexibility. Until Verenium can demonstrate its ability to produce ethanol at a profit, investors are advised to stay away from the stock. Furthermore, the field of cellulosic ethanol is quickly becoming very competitive. It is unlikely that all of the companies in the field will be able to survive in their present form.

Biofuel Companies

XNL	COMPANY	Xethanol Corporation
	SYMBOL	XNL
	TRADING MARKET	AMEX
	ADDRESS	1185 Avenue of the Americas, 20th Floor New York, NY 10036
	PHONE	646-723-4000
	CEO	David R. Ames
	WEB	*www.xethanol.com*

DESCRIPTION Xethanol produces and markets ethanol. The company also claims that it intends to optimize the use of biomass and convert a variety of products—including citrus peels—into ethanol. A key component of the company's strategy is to manufacture facilities in close proximity to major urban markets in the United States. Xethanol went public in 2006 in a reverse merger.

REASONS TO BE BULLISH
► The company increased sales from $4.3 million in 2005 to $11 million in 2006.

REASONS TO BE BEARISH
► Xethanol is not profitable and lost $20 million in 2006. Furthermore, it has only $18 million on hand, suggesting that by the end of 2007, the company will need to go back to investors to raise money. The company's founders have a spotty business history and have allegedly engaged in questionable ethical behavior in the past.
► Xethanol has a history of exploiting headlines regard ethanol, cellulosic ethanol, and other emerging biofuels by issuing misleading press releases. To date, few of the company's promises have panned out.
► For a company that claims to be on the cutting edge of science, Xethanol has a very small research and development budget, few scientists, and no real proof of any progress.
► Compared with other ethanol companies, it is very small and will not likely be able to compete.

continued

WHAT TO WATCH FOR   The company has indicated that it hopes to have a second ethanol facility operational by the end of 2007. If it can achieve this very modest goal, it is possible that the company could become a more legitimate—albeit still very small—ethanol producer.

CONCLUSION   Bearish. Investors are strongly encouraged to stay away from Xethanol. Its financial losses and small size do not suggest that it will be competitive any time in the foreseeable future.

Conclusion

Of all the renewable energy categories—wind, solar, etc.—hand-icapping the biofuels area is the most difficult. As mentioned in the introduction, what the government does or does not do in the years ahead is likely to be just as important as any commercial or technological breakthrough. Therefore, investors are strongly advised to monitor government activity.

Beyond that, however, I see the industry breaking down in the following way. In the very near term (2008 to 2009), corn ethanol will remain "king of the biofuels" and production will increase, but that industry will also undergo a major consolidation as larger and more efficient companies squeeze out the smaller and less productive producers.

Then sometime around 2010, cellulosic ethanol will appear on the scene and force an ethanol industry reorganization. Companies to watch include Abengoa, Range Fuels, Iogen, and Mascoma. Over this same period, biodiesel will also grow in prominence, especially as a number of leading automotive companies begin introducing new lines of automobiles that are capable of being fueled by biodiesel.

Longer term, the picture gets even fuzzier, but given the advances being made in the field of synthetic biology, investors are advised to watch companies such as Synthetic Genomics and Amyris Biotechnologies because they could turn the biofuel industry on its head.

"Today, solar energy provides less than one-tenth of one percent of our energy needs. As solar technology progresses, this figure will grow exponentially."

—Richard Smalley, Nobel-winning chemist

Chapter Five

Solar: Heating Up or Flaming Out?

Since 2004, the value of solar companies has soared from just under $1 billion to over $67 billion. Such a rapid ascent naturally raises the question of whether solar is the "next big thing" or merely this decade's equivalent of the dot-com craze—a comparison, I might add, that has been aided in part by the large number of solar IPOs that have been filed in the past few years.

Solar proponents dismiss the latter comparison and note that unlike Internet start-up stocks, solar companies are actually producing a tangible product and a good many companies (although not all) are profitable. They add that solar cell production has increased at an annualized rate of 40 percent for the past decade, and most analysts expect that growth to continue at comparable rates for at least the next decade. According to Clean Edge, the solar industry is expected to mushroom from a $15 billion industry in 2006 to over $60 billion by 2016.

Solar advocates also argue that demand will continue to exceed supply for some time and are fond of mentioning how Google, Microsoft, and DuPont have all caught the solar bug and installed solar panels at their corporate headquarters in the past year. They also point out that no less a retailing power than Wal-Mart has issued a request-for-proposal to install up to 100 MW of solar panels at its stores all across America. That such a bell-wether company has embraced solar energy, solar proponents argue, is proof positive that the technology has arrived.

Solar skeptics, however, are not nearly as optimistic. Whenever proponents point out that solar energy is a clean, abundant, reliable, and free source of energy (a favorite quote is "more sunlight strikes the earth in an hour than the world consumes in a year"), opponents are quick to counter that in spite of these facts and the industry's extraordinary growth over the past decade, solar power still accounts for less than one-tenth of one percent of the world's energy supply.

They then note that the continued growth predicted by solar's fans is not ordained, for the simple reason that the entire industry is still heavily reliant on government subsidies. Much of the growth over the past few years has been driven by extremely generous tax incentives in Germany and Japan. And in the United States, which is expected to represent the next growth market for the industry, the federal government is offering a 30 percent tax credit—as are some states including California, which has a Million Solar Roofs initiative and is subsidizing solar cells to the tune of $3.2 billion alone.

As these skeptics point out, such government largesse does not indicate a viable, self-sustaining industry, and if the incentives are curtailed or eliminated, the industry could come to a virtual standstill. (Personally, I believe such an outcome is unlikely, but investors must remain cognizant that solar energy is still a relatively small industry and it will be battling in the halls of Congress against some very powerful and entrenched energy industry interest groups.)

What, then, is an investor to make of such diametrically opposed viewpoints? One perspective is that the truth lies somewhere between the two extremes: solar does have great potential, but it will likely be some time before it can compete head-to-head with other energy sources in terms of cost and begin approaching anything near the capacity of those other energy sources. (It is worth noting, though, that the oil, natural gas, coal, and nuclear industries also receive government subsidies. In the event the government begins calculating environmental costs, solar could quickly become more economically viable.)

In the near term (through 2009), the majority of the solar industry's focus will be on two things: improving the efficiency conversion rate of silicon solar cells and reducing the amount of silicon used in those cells. As to the former point, today most silicon solar cells—which represent between 90 and 95 percent of all solar cells currently sold—have an energy conversion rate of between 13 and 18 percent, meaning that only 13 to 18 percent of the sunlight that strikes a cell is actually converted into usable energy. A number of companies are dedicating a good deal of time, money, and effort to this effort, including SunPower Corporation, which in early 2007 announced it had created a cell with a 22 percent conversion rate. It is an area that investors are strongly encouraged to monitor because an advance in this area could cause a company to gain market share very quickly.

Solar companies are also dedicating an extraordinary amount of effort into reducing the amount of silicon used in the production of each cell. This is because between 40 and 50 percent of the cost of producing silicon solar cells is attributed to the price of silicon. And silicon, which is also used heavily in the production of semiconductors, has come under extraordinary pricing pressure the past few years as the demand for silicon solar cells has soared. This has been good news for companies that supply the silicon wafers, such as MEMC Electronic Materials, but bad news for the producers who have seen their margins hammered by the rising prices. One solution has been for solar companies to sign long-term supply contracts with these suppliers, the advantage being that they will have a secure supply of silicon and can thus better manage their costs.

Another manner in which solar companies have attempted to protect their margins is by creating economies of scale in their manufacturing processes. In just the past year, Suntech Power, Sharp, and Kyocera have all announced major expansions in the number of solar cells they will be producing.

In many ways these three factors—improving the efficiency conversion rate, reducing the amount of silicon, and achieving economies of scale—all favor the large solar manufacturers who have the resources, industry connections, and size necessary to achieve these goals. Therefore, investors are encouraged to pay close attention to the five largest solar companies—Sharp, Sanyo, Kyocera, Q-Cells, and Suntech Power. They are likely to be formidable players in the foreseeable future, and as the industry shakes out in the years ahead and goes through a consolidation, investors can look for most of these companies to be among those still standing.

Go Thin to Win?

In the mid-term (2010 to 2013), however, the dynamics of the industry could shift significantly. That is because new alternative solar technologies are on the verge of gaining widespread commercial acceptance. As mentioned earlier, silicon solar cells today account for over 90 percent of the market. The remaining percentage is thin-film solar cells.

Typically these thin-film solar cells are made from strong light-absorbing materials such as cadmium telluride (CdTe) or copper indium gallium di-selenide (CIGS) and are much less expensive than their silicon counterparts because they require very little silicon. They also have the advantage of being amenable to large-area deposition—a characteristic that enables them to be manufactured less expensively.

The downside to thin-film solar cells is twofold. First, thin-films don't last nearly as long as silicon solar cells, and this often means that they don't provide the same type of long-term payback as silicon solar cells. Second, and perhaps more important, they are not nearly as energy efficient as silicon solar cells—meaning that thin-film solar cells must cover more space to produce a comparable amount of power as a silicon cell. For many applications, such as powering a home or business that has a limited amount of space, this is an obvious disadvantage. But for other applications, such as large-scale solar farms, it is a nonissue.

What matters for these applications is the cost per watt of energy produced. Put another way, if a solar cell can be made large enough and at a low enough cost, even though it is not as long lasting or as efficient as a silicon solar cell, it may still be more cost-effective.

Investors need to keep a close eye on whether thin-film producers can increase the efficiency of their cells while keeping their cost down. If they can, not only could thin-films become a more attractive option as a large-scale source of power but they could also begin replacing silicon solar cells for many uses. Some analysts have suggested that the real question is no longer *if* thin-film solar cells can replace silicon cells but rather *when*.

To this end, investors are encouraged to pay close attention to both the research efforts and the manufacturing plans of leading solar companies as they pertain to the development of thin-film solar cells. For instance, in just the past year Suntech Power, General Electric, and Sharp have all announced large-scale plans to move into the thin-film space. This suggests they understand how the technology might transform their business.

Alas, the competition won't end there. A large number of small but very promising private solar companies are also investigating new technologies and manufacturing techniques. For example, Konarka Technologies is seeking to coat nanoscale particles of titanium dioxide with light-absorbing dyes and then incorporating those materials directly into polymers to create plastic solar cells. HelioVolt, another private company, is seeking to incorporate thin-films directly into building tiles and materials, a process referred to as building integrated photovoltaics (BIPV). If successful, it will mean that building materials will simply double as solar cells and that there will be no installation costs.

Nanosolar, another intriguing company, has received over $100 million in venture capital funding. It has devised a cocktail of alcohol and nanoscale compounds that it claims can be sprayed on a metal foil to produce flexible solar cells, which can then be manufactured in a roll-to-roll process. In late 2006, the company announced plans to construct a manufacturing facility capable of producing 430 MW of solar energy a year. To understand the significance of this scale, it is worth noting that as recently as the year 2000 the entire manufacturing output of the solar energy industry was just 500 MW.

With this short primer on solar technology, let's take a look at some of the leading publicly traded and privately owned solar companies:

Solar Companies

AMAT	COMPANY	Applied Materials
	SYMBOL	AMAT
	TRADING MARKET	NASDAQ
	ADDRESS	3050 Bowers Avenue Santa Clara, CA 95052
	PHONE	408-727-5555
	CEO	Michael Splinter
	WEB	*www.appliedmaterials.com*

DESCRIPTION   Applied Materials is regarded as a "pick 'n' shovel" investment player in the cleantech arena because in early 2006 the company purchased Applied Films, a supplier of thin-film deposition equipment. This equipment is expected to play a big role in facilitating the production of thin-film solar cells. (The term "pick 'n' shovel" refers to the idea that among the winning companies of any boom will be those that supply the equipment to the field. Its name comes from the idea that during the Gold Rush of 1849 the first companies to profit were those that sold picks and shovels to the golddiggers.)

REASONS TO BE BULLISH

► In 2007, Moser Baer announced plans to build a large-scale, 250 MW thin-film production facility and announced that Applied Materials would be developing and installing the production line. Later in the year, the company was awarded a similar, albeit smaller contract, to supply T-Solar Global of Spain with a thin-film solar module production line.

► In 2006, the company sold $200 million worth of solar cell manufacturing machines. It expects this figure to grow to $500 million by the end of 2007.

► In the summer of 2007, Applied Materials acquired HCT Shaping Systems, which makes precision wafering systems for the solar industry.

► To the extent that the thin-film industry grows and comes to represent a larger percentage of all solar sales, Applied Materials will be well positioned for growth.

continued

REASONS TO BE BEARISH

► Applied Materials is primarily an equipment supplier for the semiconductor industry. Even if it grows to $500 million in 2007, its solar business would, at that level, still only represent 5 percent of its overall revenue. As such, the company's stock will remain more closely tied to the cyclical nature of the semiconductor industry for some time.

► Silicon solar cells still dominate the solar market, and thin-film is likely to remain a niche market through 2010.

WHAT TO WATCH FOR   Applied Materials' growth in the solar market will largely be determined by how quickly advances in thin-film solar cell technology allow the technology to be pushed into the commercial market. Any advances in nanotechnology or plastic/polymer production introduced in 2008 and 2009 will be a positive sign for Applied Materials, because such advances are expected to aid thin-film solar cell production.

CONCLUSION   Bullish. The company cannot be regarded as a pure cleantech investment; however, investors who are interested in adding some diversity to their portfolio or who are intrigued at the prospect of adding a company with a relatively low price-to-earnings ratio (16) should consider the stock.

Solar Companies

ASTI	COMPANY	Ascent Solar Technologies, Inc.
	SYMBOL	ASTI
	TRADING MARKET	NASDAQ
	ADDRESS	8120 Shaffer Parkway Littleton, CO 80127-4107
	PHONE	303-420-1141
	CEO	Matthew Foster
	WEB	*www.ascentsolartech.com*

DESCRIPTION   Ascent Solar is a development-stage company engaged in the production and commercialization of thin-film copper indium gallium di-selenide photovoltaic modules. Unlike most other solar companies, Ascent Solar intends to target its solar cells for the satellite and high-altitude aircraft market.

REASONS TO BE BULLISH

► Ascent Solar is focused on niche markets—satellites and high-altitude aircraft—and thus faces less competition than other solar companies.

► In 2007, Ascent received a $105 million investment from Norsk Hydro, a Norwegian oil and gas producer to help develop its technology. Norsk Hydro now owns 23 percent of the company.

► The same year, the company received two separate grants. The first was from the U.S. Department of Energy and was directed toward helping the company increase the conversion efficiency of its solar cells to 20 percent. The second was from the U.S. Air Force to develop a new material for inclusion in its solar cells.

► Lockheed Martin is reportedly considering using Ascent's solar cells on a high-altitude aircraft that is expected to launch in 2009.

► The company is reportedly developing a process that will integrate solar cells directly into the manufacturing process. This will allow the cells to come off the assembly line in the form of fully functioning solar modules. This labor-saving step will likely appeal to both home-buyers and building installers because it will reduce costs.

► Ascent is using the money from Norsk Hydro and its 2006 IPO to begin construction of a 1.5 MW production facility.

continued

REASONS TO BE BEARISH

► As a development-stage company, Ascent Solar is not yet profitable and is unlikely to be until 2009 at the earliest.

► The market for solar cells for satellites and high-altitude aircraft is limited. To be competitive long term, Ascent may need to develop thin-film technology that can compete with other thin-film producers.

WHAT TO WATCH FOR In the near term, investors are encouraged to monitor the status of Ascent's pilot production facility. It is expected to be producing 1.5 MW of modules by early 2008 and company officials have suggested that that level could increase to 100 MW by 2010. Another promising indicator will be news that Ascent has increased the conversion efficiency of its cells to the 20 percent range.

CONCLUSION Bullish. Ascent will likely be a volatile stock, but investors with a tolerance for stocks that have a high risk-to-reward ratio are encouraged to consider Ascent. In the short term, the company can earn real revenue by focusing on the high-altitude aircraft/satellite market; longer term, if it finds a way to integrate its solar technology directly into building materials, it could expand into a very large and growing home and business construction market.

Solar Companies

CSIQ	COMPANY	Canadian Solar Inc.
	SYMBOL	CSIQ
	TRADING MARKET	NASDAQ
	ADDRESS	199 Lushan Road, Suzhou Jiangsu, China 215129
	PHONE	86-512-669008088
	CEO	Dr. Shawn Qu
	WEB	*www.csisolar.com*

DESCRIPTION In spite of its name, Canadian Solar is actually a Chinese company. (It is only incorporated in Canada; it does all of its manufacturing in China.) It is a vertically integrated manufacturer of monocrystalline and multicrystalline solar cells, solar modules, and custom-designed solar application products.

REASONS TO BE BULLISH

► Canadian Solar expects to produce 64 MW of solar cells in 2007, and demand for its products currently exceeds supply. (In April, the company signed a deal with JA Solar to supply it with solar cells in order to ensure that it could meet growing demand.)

► In June of 2007, the company broke ground on a new 250 MW manufacturing facility in China. It is expected to be completed in late 2007.

► The company signed a large $250 million contract with Deutsche Solar to supply it with silicon wafer for twelve years, ensuring that it has a long-term supply of silicon.

► Canadian Solar is branching into the building integrated photovoltaic (BIPV) market and has even supplied a solar glass roof system to a large company in China.

► In 2007, the company signed a $50 million deal with Amur Energy Division of Spain to supply it with solar cells.

► Canadian Solar operates one of the largest silicon reclaiming business centers in the world. As a result, it has a modest advantage over other solar competitors in that it has access to lower-cost silicon for a portion of its manufacturing needs.

continued

Canadian Solar Inc. continued

REASONS TO BE BEARISH

► Canadian Solar remains highly dependent on the German market for sales. In 2007 the German market began to soften, and this had an adverse impact on the company's revenues. To the extent the German market continues to soften or the German government reduces its generous solar subsidies, it can cause severe problems for the company.

► To date, the company has provided little information on the efficiency of its solar cells, suggesting that it is not as efficient as some of its other competitors, such as Trina Solar or Solarfun.

WHAT TO WATCH FOR   Investors are encouraged to watch for four things: (1) news that Canadian Solar is expanding away from the German market and into other markets; (2) progress in its development of solar cells with a higher energy conversion rate; (3) indications that its new 250 MW manufacturing plant will be able to produce at full capacity in 2008; and (4) signs that its BIPV business is growing.

CONCLUSION   Neutral. Canadian Solar is growing quickly but the company needs to get its new manufacturing facility operational before investors should consider investing. Investors should also wait until the company offers more information about how its solar cells will stand out in today's crowded commercial marketplace by either making them more efficient or incorporating them into BIPV.

Solar Companies

DSTI	COMPANY	DayStar Technologies, Inc.
	SYMBOL	DSTI
	TRADING MARKET	NASDAQ
	ADDRESS	13 Corporate Drive Halfmoon, NY 12065
	PHONE	518-383-4600
	CEO	Stephen Deluca
	WEB	*www.daystartech.com*

DESCRIPTION DayStar Technologies is engaged in the development, manufacturing, and marketing of copper indium gallium di-selenide thin-film solar cells. The company's main product, TerraFoil, has a stainless-steel base and can be integrated directly into building construction materials such as roofing and siding.

REASONS TO BE BULLISH
► DayStar is reportedly developing a next-generation product that will have a conversation efficiency ratio as high as 10 percent.

REASONS TO BE BEARISH
► In the first quarter of 2007, the company reported a staggering loss of $18 million and it is burning cash at a rate of over $1.2 million a month. Even with the help of a $4 million bridge financing loan that it received in May of 2007, the company will likely be out of money in less than a year.
► DayStar has indicated that it will use its money to construct a manufacturing facility in California to produce next-generation solar cells, yet there is no indication that it has anywhere near the financial resources to accomplish this goal. At a minimum, it appears DayStar will either need to secure a lot more money (and dilute existing shareholder value) or face bankruptcy as early as 2008.
► Even if the company's facility begins producing the next-generation solar cells, there is no guarantee that the product will be competitive with other thin-film solar cells being produced by such companies as Miasolé or Nanosolar.

continued

WHAT TO WATCH FOR   Investors need to monitor the company's cash-burn rate. Additionally, the company has indicated that it plans for the new facility to produce 50 MW of solar cells by the end of 2008. Until this facility is actually built and is then producing 50 MW of solar cells with a conversation rate of at least 10 percent, investors are cautioned to stay away from this stock.

CONCLUSION   Bearish. A lack of money and a technology that appears to be inferior to those being developed by its competitors make DayStar Technologies a very risky stock. Investors interested in thin-film solar cells are encouraged to consider an investment in First Solar or, alternatively, wait to see if Miasolé, HelioVolt, or Nanosolar goes public.

ENER	COMPANY	Energy Conversion Devices (also known as ECD Ovonics)
	SYMBOL	ENER
	TRADING MARKET	NASDAQ
	ADDRESS	2956 Waterview Drive Rochester Hills, MI 48309
	PHONE	248-293-0440
	CEO	Mark D. Morelli
	WEB	*www.ovonic.com*

DESCRIPTION   Founded by Stanford Ovshinsky, who retired in 2007, Energy Conversion Devices invents, designs, develops, manufactures, and commercializes a variety of products for the alternative energy generation market, including thin-film solar cells, nickel metal hydride (NiMH) batteries, and fuel cell components. The company recently reorganized itself into two divisions: United Solar Ovonic and Ovonic Materials.

REASONS TO BE BULLISH

► ECD owns 50 percent of Cobasys (Chevron owns the remaining half), which is the only U.S.-based manufacturer that offers NiMH battery systems for hybrid cars. Its batteries are already being used in General Motors's Saturn Vue hybrid sports utility vehicle.

► The United Solar Ovonic division is profitable, and because it employs a thin-film process that uses little polysilicon, its cells are much less expensive to manufacture than traditional crystalline solar cells. As of 2007, the division was producing over 100 MW of solar cells and intends to increase that to 300 MW by 2010.

► United Solar Ovonic has received a $19 million grant from the U.S. Department of Energy to develop low-cost thin-film building integrated photovoltaic systems (BIPV).

► ECD had close to $400 million cash on hand at the end of 2007.

► The company has a very strong portfolio of intellectual property, and its management team (including Roger Stempel, the former CEO of General Motors, who is now chairman of the board) has done an excellent job of forming constructive partnerships with leading corporations.

continued

Energy Conversion Devices continued

REASONS TO BE BEARISH

► As remarkable as it may seem, ECD has lost money in forty-three of the forty-seven years it has been in existence, and the company is not projecting itself to be profitable again until 2009.

► The company's solar technology will face a great deal of competition from other solar companies, and if the price of silicon drops in the years ahead the cost advantage of thin-film solar cells may fade away.

► To date, ECD has invested over $100 million in hydrogen systems but has little to show for its efforts.

► In the battery area, Toyota is using batteries from Panasonic. This suggests that Cobasys doesn't necessarily have a lock on the hybrid battery market. Other companies such as A123 and Altair Nanotechnologies are also developing competing battery technology.

WHAT TO WATCH FOR   In the near term (2008 to 2009), the company's success will be dependent upon its ability to increase the margins on its solar business and ramp up production of its thin-film plant to a capacity of 300 MW. If it can achieve these things, the company will be well positioned to become profitable. Longer term, investors should monitor ECD's ability both to continue improving its NiMH battery technology and to perfect its fuel cell technology.

CONCLUSION   Bullish. In spite of the company's long history of unprofitability, the fact that its solar division is finally profitable and growing fast suggests that the company is within reach of consistent profitability. Provided no other thin-film solar company (e.g. Nanosolar, Miasolé, HelioVolt, and Suntech Power) develops a cheaper or more efficient solar cell, ECD is well positioned for future growth. Investors with a higher penchant for risk are encouraged to consider an investment.

COMPANY	Energy Innovations
INVESTORS	Private (not publicly available)
ADDRESS	130 W. Union Street Pasadena, CA 91103
PHONE	626-585-6900
CEO	Bill Gross
WEB	*www.energyinnovations.com*

DESCRIPTION   Energy Innovations is a development-stage solar energy company. Its long-term goal is to develop solar systems that are priced at two-thirds the cost of existing photovoltaic systems.

WHY IT IS DISRUPTIVE   Unlike almost every other solar cell system, Energy Innovations is attempting to construct its system out of an array of twenty-five moveable mirrors that concentrate solar energy on a focused surface area. The technology maximizes the energy it receives from the sun by getting more energy from a smaller number of solar cells; and by relying on a computerized system that moves the mirrors to match the angle of the sun, the system is able to stay productive later into the day (when most businesses and homeowners are demanding the most energy).

WHAT TO WATCH FOR   The company installed its first 1.6 MW system at Google's corporate headquarters. It will now need to demonstrate that it can build upon this success. Equally important, Energy Innovations will need to make good on its promise to deliver a solar system that is cheaper than its more conventional competitors. Unless the company can deliver a shorter payback time for customers, it is unlikely that many businesses or homeowners will risk buying this newer technology.

CONCLUSION   Bullish. Although Energy Innovations has experienced a number of setbacks in bringing a product to market, the company has been unusually open about its problems. And these setbacks are far from being failures; the company appears to be learning more about what is and isn't working, which bodes well for its future prospects because with each step it is getting closer to a practical product. Energy Innovations is a private company and will likely remain so for some time, but all investors in solar energy should nevertheless keep track of its developments, because the company has the potential to change how solar systems are manufactured.

Solar Companies

ESLR	COMPANY	Evergreen Solar
	SYMBOL	ESLR
	TRADING MARKET	NASDAQ
	ADDRESS	138 Bartlett Street Marlboro, MA 01752
	PHONE	508-357-2221
	CEO	Richard M. Feldt
	WEB	*www.evergreensolar.com*

DESCRIPTION Evergreen Solar develops, manufactures, and markets solar power products distinguished by its String Ribbon technology. String Ribbon is an efficient process for manufacturing crystalline silicon wafers and, according to the company, yields over twice as many solar cells per pound of silicon as conventional methods.

REASONS TO BE BULLISH

- ▶ Because the company's String Ribbon technology yields more solar cells per pound of silicon than conventional methods, Evergreen has less exposure to fluctuations in the price of silicon and is thus better positioned to maintain healthier operating margins.
- ▶ Evergreen Solar continues to improve upon the technology. Its second-generation 3.2-inch-wide ribbon has a 33 percent faster pulling speed, and this doubles furnace productivity. Future generations of the technology are expected to make further improvements in both speed and productivity.
- ▶ In 2007, the company signed a major extension of its sales agreement with SunEdison (North America's leading solar energy service provider). This brings the total value of contracts with SunEdison to over $500 million.
- ▶ The same year, Evergreen received a multi-million investment from DC Chemical of Korea, along with a pledge to supply it with polysilicon from 2008 through 2014.
- ▶ Evergreen also has a number of agreements with other energy providers totaling an additional $500 million.
- ▶ Since 2006, Evergreen has a strategic partnership, dubbed EverQ, with Q-Cells of Germany and Renewable Energy Corporation of Norway. The partnerships position it well to compete in both North America and Europe.

continued

► By the end of 2007, a second EverQ facility is expected to bring the total production capacity of Evergreen-branded panels to over 100 megawatts.

► In mid-2007, the company announced that it would be building a new $150 million manufacturing plant in Massachusetts and would be receiving $44 million in grants and low-interest loans from the state government to help finance the construction of the plant.

REASONS TO BE BEARISH

► The company has yet to achieve an annual profit and is not expected to do so until 2008 at the earliest.

► While Q-Cells and Renewable Energy both utilize Evergreen's String Ribbon technology, the bulk of the company's revenues come from its Massachusetts-based manufacturing facility, which is significantly smaller than the joint EverQ facility in Germany.

WHAT TO WATCH FOR   Evergreen will need to continue to focus on improving its technology, lowering its manufacturing costs, and increasing production capacity. The deal with SunPower is a good start toward the latter goal, but it will need a lot more capacity in order to be competitive with many of the other solar companies that are already profitable.

CONCLUSION   Bearish. The company will need to achieve extraordinary growth in order to become competitive. Longer term, its String Ribbon technology is vulnerable to advances in thin-film solar technology.

Solar Companies

FSLR	COMPANY	First Solar, Inc.
	SYMBOL	FSLR
	TRADING MARKET	NASDAQ
	ADDRESS	4050 East Cotton Center Boulevard, Building 6 Phoenix, AZ 85040
	PHONE	602-414-9300
	CEO	Bruce Sohn
	WEB	*www.firstsolar.com*

DESCRIPTION   First Solar designs, manufactures, and sells solar modules. Unlike most other solar companies, First Solar manufactures its solar cells out of a multicrystalline thin-film structure that utilizes cadmium telluride (CdTe) semiconductor material to convert sunlight into electricity.

REASONS TO BE BULLISH

► First Solar increased its revenues by almost 400 percent in 2006 and it expects to double in size again in 2007. In the first quarter of 2007, the company also reported its first profit.

► Because CdTe can be sprayed on glass to create solar cells, it is significantly cheaper to manufacture than traditional silicon solar cells.

► CdTe has other benefits as well. It is less susceptible to cell temperature increases and absorbs low and diffuse light more efficiently than other materials. Because it is a "direct bandgap" semiconductor, it converts sunlight into electricity more efficiently than indirect bandgap materials.

► First Solar continues to make great progress in lowering the cost of manufacturing its solar cells. In late 2006, its cells cost $1.42 per watt. By mid-2007, the company lowered the cost to $1.25, and expects to lower it below $1.00 per watt by 2010. (Conventional electricity costs in the neighborhood of $.75. Therefore, if First Solar continues to make progress, solar could be cost-competitive with fossil fuel sources within a few years.)

► In 2007, the company began construction of a 120 MW facility in Malaysia. By 2008, First Solar expects to be producing 1,000 MW of solar modules annually through its production facilities in Germany, the United States, and Malaysia.

continued

First Solar, Inc. continued

► It also recently signed a multi-year contract with SunEdison to supply that company with solar modules.

REASONS TO BE BEARISH
► At the time of this writing, First Solar had a price-to-earnings ratio of 212 and had more than sevenfold in price from its original IPO price of $25. Even after its 2008 estimated earnings are factored in, the company is still trading at an extremely high forward P/E ratio of 100.
► Although lower in price, First Solar's solar modules are not as efficient as silicon solar cells. If the price of silicon drops, the company could lose some of its cost advantage.

WHAT TO WATCH FOR   First Solar will need to continue to lower the cost per watt of its solar modules. If it can reach the $1.00 per watt level, that will be a major milestone and a very bullish signal for the company—provided, that is, that another company such as United Solar Ovonic, Nanosolar, or Miasolé doesn't reach this goal first.

CONCLUSION   Bullish. First Solar has a lofty price-to-earnings ratio, but its extraordinary growth can partly justify this valuation. Investors with a higher tolerance for risk and a five- to ten-year outlook are encouraged to consider this stock as a long-term buy-and-hold.

Solar Companies

COMPANY	HelioVolt Corporation
INVESTORS	New Enterprise Associates
ADDRESS	8201 East Riverside Drive, Suite 600 Austin, TX 78744-1604
PHONE	512-767-6000
CEO	Bill Stanbery
WEB	*www.heliovolt.com*

DESCRIPTION   HelioVolt is a development-stage company seeking to apply thin-film photovoltaic coatings made of copper indium gallium di-selenide (CIGS) directly onto building construction materials.

WHY IT IS DISRUPTIVE   Dubbed FASST, HelioVolt's proprietary process can reportedly produce layers that are 100 times thinner than existing silicon solar cells. Moreover, the process is said to be ten times faster than other thin-film processes. The technology can also print these solar coatings directly onto various substrates including steel, glass, and polymer. If true, this implies that any number of building materials could be made to double as solar cells. It would also remove many of the marginal costs typically associated with other solar cells—notably, converting the solar cells into solar modules and then installing those modules onto a building. With HelioVolt's FASST technology, all of these costs would be eliminated because the solar cell is, in effect, the building material. The company's technology has received numerous awards, including being recognized by the *Wall Street Journal* and *Time* magazine for having one of the most promising technologies of this decade. In August 2007, it secured $77 million in venture capital funding to begin executing on its manufacturing plans.

WHAT TO WATCH FOR   Nanosolar, Miasolé, and others are also developing thin-film CIGS solar cells. To survive, HelioVolt will have to prove that it can manufacture building materials coated with its technology and that it can increase the efficiency conversion rate of its solar cells. The company wants to have a manufacturing facility operational by the end of 2007 and be producing materials sometime in 2008. To this end, it has begun to hire a variety of experienced executives to oversee the operation.

continued

CONCLUSION   Bullish. HelioVolt appears to possess a very disruptive technology. Until it can actually begin manufacturing materials, however, it is just another company with a promising technology. If it successfully produces building materials that double as solar cells and is manufacturing between 20 and 40 MW of solar cells by 2009, investors can expect the company to go public in 2009 or 2010. In the event that it does, investors with a high tolerance for risk are encouraged to invest in the company because it is the type of company that not only could change how solar cells are built but could transform the building construction business by allowing builders to start using photovoltaic building materials that incorporate photovoltaics.

Solar Companies

JASO	COMPANY	JA Solar
	SYMBOL	JASO
	TRADING MARKET	NASDAQ
	ADDRESS	Jinglong Street, Jinglong Group Industrial Park Ningjin, China 055550
	PHONE	86-31-95800760
	CEO	Samuel Yang
	WEB	*www.jasolar.com*

DESCRIPTION　JA Solar designs, manufactures, and sells monocrystalline solar cells primarily in China, although it also has customers in Europe, Asia, and the United States. In February of 2007, the company was publicly listed on the NASDAQ stock exchange.

REASONS TO BE BULLISH

► From no revenues in 2005, the company grew to $90 million in revenues in 2006 and expects $280 million in 2007. In 2008, the company expects to grow an additional 40 percent to nearly $400 million in revenue.

► In addition to revenue growth, JA Solar is already profitable. Among its peers in the solar industry, it offers the best return on equity.

► Its parent company, the Jinglong Group, is China's largest maker of silicon wafers, suggesting that it has relatively secure and affordable access to silicon wafers. This, in turn, should allow the company to post better operating margins than some of its leading competitors.

► The quality of JA Solar's solar cells appears to be quite high, and it offers a twenty-five-year warranty on its cells, which is attracting additional customers.

REASONS TO BE BEARISH

► Although its relationship with the Jinglong Group is beneficial, it has only secured supplies of silicon through 2007. A substantial increase in price in silicon could leave it vulnerable to competitors who have secured longer-term silicon supply contracts at more favorable rates.

continued

► The company only specializes in the production of solar cells. This practice could insulate the company somewhat from its customers and might hurt its ability to market its solar cells. Other competitors such as Suntech Power and Trina Solar are seeking to become more full service solar providers.

WHAT TO WATCH FOR   Look for JA Solar to secure long-term supplies of silicon for 2008 and beyond. If it does, the company should be able to expand its production capacity beyond the 100 MW level in 2008. Investors will also want to look for evidence that JA Solar is improving the efficiency level of its solar cells in a range that will allow it to stay competitive with its peers.

CONCLUSION   Bullish. The company's access to silicon wafers through the Jinglong Group, in combination with its impressive operating margins and return on equity, suggests that it is a company to be taken seriously. Moreover, as a Chinese company, it is well positioned to benefit from China's continued economic expansion and growing commitment to develop clean energy sources.

Solar Companies

COMPANY	Konarka Technologies
INVESTORS	Draper Fisher Jurvetson, Zero Stage Capital, Chevron, Eastman Chemical, and numerous others
ADDRESS	116 John Street, Suite 12, Third Floor Lowell, MA 01852
PHONE	978-569-1400
CEO	Rick Hess
WEB	*www.konarkatech.com*

DESCRIPTION Konarka utilizes nanomaterials and conductive polymers to manufacture light-activated power plastics that are inexpensive, lightweight, flexible, and versatile. In 2004, it purchased Siemens' solar cell research. The company expects to have a product on the market in 2008.

WHY IT IS DISRUPTIVE Konarka is developing plastic rolls that can be embedded with titanium dioxide nanoparticles, which more efficiently convert natural and indoor light into electricity. The company's manufacturing process reportedly allows photoreactive materials to be printed or coated directly onto flexible substrates using roll-to-roll manufacturing—similar to how newspaper is printed on large rolls of paper. The company hopes first to develop flexible solar coatings for laptop computers and mobile phones. Mid-term, it is working on producing a "solar" tent for the U.S. Army that would produce its own energy, and longer term, it is working on inexpensive, lightweight rolls of solar cells that could cover a home or business, thus allowing customers to use less power from the existing grid.

Konarka's proprietary technology also offers a few other advantages over competitors' thin-film processes. For instance, its photovoltaic materials can be produced with different colors and varying degrees of translucency. This could enable the technology to be customized for new products and markets. The process also is environmentally friendly (no toxic solvents) and does not require manufacturers to buy or install any new equipment (it uses existing coating and printing technologies).

continued

Konarka Technologies continued

WHAT TO WATCH FOR   BP Solar, Nanosolar, HelioVolt, and First Solar are all working on related technologies, so there is no guarantee that Konarka will develop the best or most practical product. However, Konarka's partnerships with Chevron, France's largest electrical utility company, and the U.S. Department of Defense are all very promising. If computer, laptop, or cell phone manufacturers begin incorporating Konarka's technology into next-generation devices or if the company enters into a partnership with a major manufacturer to produce solar "shingles" for roofs, it will be an even more positive sign. The most positive indicator, however, will be Konarka's ability to decrease the cost of energy produced per watt.

CONCLUSION   Bullish. Unlike most other thin-film solar companies, Konarka has an interim path to profitability if its solar cells can be used to supplement the power supply of existing mobile-communication devices. Investors should definitely keep this company on their radar screen for a future IPO.

Solar Companies

KYO	COMPANY	Kyocera Corporation
	SYMBOL	KYO
	TRADING MARKET	NYSE
	ADDRESS	6 Takeda Tobadono-cho, Fushimi-ku Kyoto, 612-8501, Japan
	PHONE	81-7-5604-3500
	CEO	Noburo Nakamura
	WEB	*www.kyocera.com*

DESCRIPTION   Kyocera Corporation is a large Japanese conglomerate that develops, manufactures, and sells telecommunications equipment and electronic components. It also owns Kyocera Solar, one of the world's largest vertically integrated producers and suppliers of solar energy products.

REASONS TO BE BULLISH

► In mid-2007, the company announced it was quadrupling the manufacturing capacity of its solar cell plant in Tijuana, Mexico, from 35 MW to 150 MW by the end of 2011. The move will help ensure that Kyocera remains competitive with low-cost manufacturers in the lucrative U.S. market.

► Kyocera has three manufacturing facilities in Japan, China, and the Czech Republic. By the end of 2011, the four facilities are expected to be producing over 500 MW of solar cells.

► Near the end of 2006, the company announced that its multicrystalline silicon solar cells had achieved a new world record in solar cell efficiency by reaching an energy conversion rate of 18.5 percent.

► Kyocera is pursuing new markets for solar cells. One of the more promising fields is solar carports. The idea is to transform parking lots into mini solar farms that can be used to reduce a company's energy bill while at the same time keeping employees' cars cool and shaded.

continued

Kyocera Corporation continued

REASONS TO BE BEARISH

► The overwhelming majority of Kyocera's business is not focused on solar cells, but rather on low-margin products such as black-and-white printers and low-end cell phones.

► As a Japan-based company, it profits are sensitive to fluctuations in the exchange rate for the yen.

► Suntech Power and other Chinese solar manufacturers will have access to cheaper labor than Kyocera.

WHAT TO WATCH FOR Kyocera Solar will need to continue to increase the efficiency of its solar cells as well as ramp up manufacturing capacity. Investors should look for news that it has increased the energy conversion rate of its multicrystalline cells to 20 percent by 2010 and that, in order to stay competitive, it has an annual production capacity of at least 500 MW sooner than 2011.

CONCLUSION Bearish. Kyocera's core business of telecommunications and electronics does not stand out from its competitors, and Kyocera Solar faces too much competition from other solar manufacturers. Investors interested in a pure-play solar investment are encouraged to consider First Solar or Suntech Power.

WFR	COMPANY	MEMC Electronic Materials Inc.
	SYMBOL	WFR
	TRADING MARKET	NASDAQ
	ADDRESS	501 Pearl Drive St. Peter, MO 63376-0008
	PHONE	636-474-5000
	CEO	Nabeel Gareeb
	WEB	*www.memc.com*

DESCRIPTION   MEMC is a global leader in the manufacture of silicon wafers and, although it primarily designs, manufactures, and provides wafers for the semiconductor industry, it also supplies a growing percentage of its silicon wafers to the solar industry.

REASONS TO BE BULLISH

► Revenues grew almost 40 percent in 2006 and an additional 25 percent in 2007. Profits were also up a comparable amount over the same period. From 2005 to 2007, the company's stock jumped from $11 to $58.

► Much of this growth has been driven by the increasing demand for silicon from solar cell manufacturers. In 2005 only 10 percent of MEMC's business came from the solar industry. Some industry analysts believe that figure could increase to 33 percent by 2012.

► In late 2006, MEMC signed a long-term deal reported to be worth between $5 billion and $6 billion to supply Suntech with solar wafers.

► The company possesses more than 500 patents and its granular silicon technology gives it a price advantage over its competitors in supplying wafers to the solar market.

► MEMC has a strong balance sheet with over $800 million cash on hand. In 2007, its management team initiated a $500 million stock repurchase plan.

continued

MEMC Electronic Materials Inc. continued

REASONS TO BE BEARISH

► In spite of the company's extraordinary growth, silicon remains a basic commodity and the industry has long been subject to boom/bust cycles. Most analysts expect that the high price of silicon wafers will lead to a surplus (due to overproduction) by mid-2008. When that happens, MEMC's profits could be hit especially hard.

► If the price of silicon does remain high, that provides an incentive for many solar cell producers to begin exploring thin-film solar technology. This, in turn, could cause more companies to aggressively pursue thin-film productions options, and that will depress silicon prices in the long term.

► MEMC faces great competition from three other large silicon wafer suppliers.

► A good portion of the company is still controlled by a private equity group, which may not always act in the individual shareholders' interest.

► Although it has a ten-year agreement with Suntech to supply the company with wafers, it is possible that the deal might fall through if silicon prices drop low enough.

WHAT TO WATCH FOR   Because the majority of its business is tied to the semi-conductor industry, investors need to understand the cyclical nature of that business. Investors should also watch for signs that the wafer market is approaching overcapacity.

CONCLUSION   Bearish. MEMC is a well-managed, strong company; however, given its price run-up between 2005 and 2007 and the cyclical nature of the industries it serves, it is hard to imagine that its stock can continue to gain appreciably.

COMPANY	Miasolé
INVESTORS	Kleiner Perkins Caufield & Byers, VantagePoint Venture Partners, Firelake Strategic Technology Fund, Garage Technology Ventures, and Nippon Kouatsu Electric Co.
ADDRESS	2590 Walsh Avenue, Santa Clara, CA 95051
PHONE	408-919-5700
CEO	David Pearce
WEB	*www.miasole.com*

DESCRIPTION   Miasolé is a private solar start-up seeking to develop thin-film polymer solar cells based on copper indium gallium di-selenide (CIGS).

WHY IT IS DISRUPTIVE   CIGS can form a direct bandgap semiconductor that can be applied to thin-films in a unique roll-to-roll process that would allow solar cells to be inexpensively printed on large plastic sheets. In addition to costing less per watt than traditional silicon solar cells, CIGS cells are efficient harvesters of photons in low-angle sunlight situations and low-light situations. Furthermore, CIGS cells are extremely low weight, flexible, very stable, and reliable. Miasolé's cells have a reported conversion rate of 15 percent and can last as long as twenty years. In 2007, Miasolé was one of a handful of companies to receive funding ($20 million) from the U.S. Department of Energy to "develop high-volume manufacturing technologies and photovoltaic component technologies." The company also received approximately $40 million from venture capital firms in 2006 to pursue its manufacturing plans.

WHAT TO WATCH FOR   Miasolé is competing directly with companies such as Nanosolar, Konarka, and HelioVolt. The key to its success will rest on its ability to execute at the manufacturing level. Company officials claimed in 2006 that Miasolé would be producing 200 MW of solar cells by 2007, but it appears to be behind that schedule. There have also been rumors that the company will go public in late 2007 or early 2008.

CONCLUSION   Neutral. Unless the company is actually manufacturing solar cells at a level approaching a 50 MW annual capacity, investors should tread very carefully. In the event Miasolé does go public, investors are encouraged to wait for signs of actual production before investing in this company. Better still, investors should first ascertain when the company expects to become profitable.

Solar Companies

COMPANY	Nanosolar
INVESTORS	Benchmark Capital, Mohr Davidow Ventures, U.S. Venture Partners, Swiss Re, OnPoint Technologies, and Google's founders (Sergey Brin and Larry Page)
ADDRESS	2440 Embarcadero Way Palo Alto, CA 94303-3313
PHONE	650-565-8891
CEO	Martin Roscheisen
WEB	*www.nanosolar.com*

DESCRIPTION Nanosolar has developed and is producing nanowires and nanoparticles that allow it to "paint" the self-assembling nanomaterials onto flexible, low-cost sheets of plastic and convert them into photovoltaic cells.

WHY IT IS DISRUPTIVE Traditional solar cells are manufactured out of silicon, which is costly, bulky, and inflexible. Nanosolar's technology offers the possibility that its cells will be 1,000 times thinner and can be manufactured 100 times faster. The technology may even lend itself to being "painted" on sides of automobiles and buses. The company received over $100 million in late 2006 to begin construction of two large-scale manufacturing facilities in San Jose, California, and in Germany. It also received a $20 million grant from the U.S. Department of Energy to develop low-cost, scalable photovoltaic systems for rooftops. This grant is on top of a $10 million grant it received from the U.S. Department of Defense's Defense Advanced Research Projects Agency (DARPA) to develop its technology in 2005. The company holds some valuable intellectual property from Sandia National Laboratories.

WHAT TO WATCH FOR Company officials have claimed that the manufacturing facility in San Jose will be capable of producing 430 MW of solar modules annually. If true, this will represent a major paradigm shift both in how solar cells are made and in their cost. The plant is expected to be operational in 2008, but it is possible that Nanosolar will encounter some obstacles in ramping up production. The company also faces considerable competition from smaller, private start-ups such as Miasolé and HelioVolt as well as larger, more established companies such as Q-Cells, First Solar, Suntech Power, General Electric, and Sharp (the largest manufacturer of silicon solar cells).

continued

Nanosolar continued

CONCLUSION   Neutral. The company is currently not available to individual investors, but if it does go public in 2008 investors will want to take a good look at where the company stands in terms of meeting its ability to produce 430 MW of cells a year. Investors will also want to check on its competitors' progress. If the former appears on track, risk-tolerant investors looking for a big payoff are encouraged to consider an investment.

QCE		
	COMPANY	Q-Cells AG
	SYMBOL	QCE
	TRADING MARKET	Frankfurt Stock Exchange
	ADDRESS	OT Thalheim Guardianstrasse 16 06766 Bitterfeld-Wolfen, Germany
	PHONE	49-3494-6699-0
	CEO	Charles Anton Milner
	WEB	*www.q-cells.com*

DESCRIPTION   Q-Cells AG is a German-based solar company engaged in the development, production, and sale of a wide variety of monocrystalline and polycrystalline solar cells. It is the largest solar manufacturer in Germany and the second largest in the world.

REASONS TO BE BULLISH
- ▶ Q-Cells is profitable and growing rapidly. It produced 255 MW of solar modules in 2006 and expects to increase that number to almost 900 MW by 2009. Over that period it expects both revenues and profits to increase by 40 percent.
- ▶ In mid-2007, Q-Cells signed a long-term supply agreement with Elkem Solar of Oslo to supply it with silicon through 2018. The contract calls for Q-Cells to receive a minimum of 2,400 tons through the period, with the right to increase the amount to 5,000 tons if necessary.
- ▶ Q-Cells has also acquired an 18 percent stake in Renewable Energy Corporation (the world's largest manufacturer of polycrystalline silicon), which gives it another nice way to profit from an increase in the demand for silicon.
- ▶ Of all the solar companies, no one is more diversified in its approach to betting on what the next-generation solar technology will be than Q-Cells. To this end, the company has invested in Solibro, a Swedish company commercializing copper indium gallium di-selenide (CIGS) thin-film technology; Brilliant 234 and Calyxo (two companies producing silicon thin-film modules); CSG Solar, an Australian company developing thin-film solar cells on glass; and, most recently, Solaria.

continued

► It is also not afraid to partner with other solar companies. In 2006, Q-Cells partnered with Evergreen Solar, and in 2007 it signed a deal with Trina Solar to supply it with modules in order to ensure that one of its manufacturing facilities operated at full capacity.

REASONS TO BE BEARISH
► The company has benefited from the German government's generous subsidies to the solar industry. If these subsidies are reduced or eliminated, it will have an adverse impact on the company.
► Like all solar companies, Q-Cells faces a great deal of competition, and it is possible that another company will develop a more efficient or less expensive solar module.

WHAT TO WATCH FOR   The company is performing admirably. Investors will want to make sure that once its new production capacity comes online, its margins continue to improve. Investors will also want to watch for signals that Q-Cells is increasing the energy conversion rates of its existing product line of solar modules.

CONCLUSION   Bullish. Q-Cells has the right approach to prospering in the rapidly growing and evolving solar market. While it has focused on increasing the production capacity of its existing silicon solar cells, the company is also placing bets on a wide variety of next-generation thin-film solar cell and solar concentration technologies in the expectation that at least one of them will pay off. Investors looking for a solid solar investment and/or who want to add some foreign stock exposure to their portfolio are encouraged to invest in this company.

Solar Companies

SOLF	COMPANY	Solarfun Power Holdings Co. Ltd.
	SYMBOL	SOLF
	TRADING MARKET	NASDAQ
	ADDRESS	666 Linyang Road Qidong, Jiangsu Province, China 226200
	PHONE	86-513-8330-7688
	CEO	Lu Yonghua
	WEB	*www.solarfun.cn*

DESCRIPTION   Solarfun manufactures and sells monocrystalline and multicrystalline solar cells primarily in China and Europe.

REASONS TO BE BULLISH

► Solarfun is expected to increase manufacturing capacity from 240 MW in 2007 to 360 MW by the end of 2008.

► In the first quarter of 2007, the company's revenues increased by 86 percent.

► In 2006, the company signed an agreement with UB Garanty of Spain to supply it with 140 MW of solar cells. The deal was worth between $40 and $50 million.

► The conversion efficiency of its cells is 16.8 percent, which is in line with industry averages.

► Solarfun has signed a long-term deal with LDK Solar to supply it with silicon.

REASONS TO BE BEARISH

► Although Solarfun's revenues increased 86 percent, this rate of increase is far less than some of its competitors'. Suntech Power, for instance, increased revenues 192 percent over the same period.

► Unlike Suntech and Trina Solar, Solarfun reported a net loss in the first half of 2007.

► Solarfun invests little in research and development, and it is not known whether the company can continue to increase the conversion rate of its solar cells necessary to keep pace with the advances others in the industry are promising.

continued

Solarfun Power Holdings Co. Ltd. continued

WHAT TO WATCH FOR   At a minimum, Solarfun will need to increase its manufacturing capacity and bolster the efficiency rate of its existing cells in order to stay competitive. Investors will want to make sure that the company is nearing a capacity of 400 MW by the end of 2008 and that the efficiency level of its cells has increased to the neighborhood of 18 percent within the same period.

CONCLUSION   Bearish. It is unlikely that all of the existing Chinese solar cell companies will be able to survive an almost inevitable industry shakeout. Little in Solarfun's literature suggests anything in either its manufacturing or its technological capabilities that distinguishes it from its larger and more established competitors. Investors interested in a strong China solar company are advised to consider Suntech Power, JA Solar, or Trina Solar.

Solar Companies

SWV		
	COMPANY	SolarWorld AG
	SYMBOL	SWV
	TRADING MARKET	Various European stock exchanges
	ADDRESS	Kurt-Schumacher-Strasse 12-14 53113 Bonn, Germany
	PHONE	49(0)228 559 20-0
	CEO	Frank Asbeck
	WEB	*www.solarworld.de/sw-eng*

DESCRIPTION   Established in 1999, SolarWorld became a major player in the solar industry in 2006 when it acquired all of Royal Dutch Shell's crystalline silicon solar cell operations. It now bills itself as a fully integrated solar company that deals with everything from producing silicon to supplying solar modules, inverters, and solar roofs.

REASONS TO BE BULLISH

► In 2006, the company reported a growth rate of 45 percent and increased revenues from 356 million euros to 515 million euros. Early figures suggest that it will grow in the neighborhood of 30 percent in 2007; and, given the growing appetite for solar energy, that rate could possibly be sustained through 2010.

► As a large company, SolarWorld can achieve the types of economies of scale necessary to be competitive. When the company's German manufacturing facility is added into the mix, it expects to produce one gigawatt (1,000 MW) of solar cells by the end of the decade.

► SolarWorld has done a good job of gaining access to long-term contracts for silicon. To the extent that the price of silicon remains high, these contracts will allow the company to compete favorably.

► In early 2007, the company acquired a large manufacturing facility in Oregon. By 2010, the company expects to be producing 500 MW of solar modules at the facility. If successful, it will be one of the largest manufacturing facilities in the United States. With its close proximity to the massive California market, the company should be able to compete favorably in this fertile territory.

continued

► In February 2007, SolarWorld entered into an agreement with Pacific Power Management to sell the company solar electric modules for a number of its upcoming installation projects.

REASONS TO BE BEARISH

► SolarWorld only purchased Shell's crystalline silicon cells business. Thus it remains vulnerable to the prospect that thin-film photovoltaic cells will become increasingly affordable, more efficient, and, quite possibly, more popular with customers.

► It will continue to face stiff competition from Q-Cells Kyocera, BP Solar, Suntech Power, and others.

WHAT TO WATCH FOR   Investors are encouraged to see whether SolarWorld maintains its strength in the German and Western European markets. Investors will also want to ensure that its planned production in the United States proceeds according to plan. A scaling back of output from the 500 MW level could signal that it is losing ground to other competitors. Longer term, investors should watch for growth in the Asian market and, beyond that, a move into thin-film solar production.

CONCLUSION   Bullish. SolarWorld has the potential to be one of the dominant players in the solar market and has done an excellent job of positioning itself for growth through 2010.

Solar Companies

SPWR	COMPANY	SunPower Corporation
	SYMBOL	SPWR
	TRADING MARKET	NASDAQ
	ADDRESS	3939 North 1st Street San Jose, CA 95134
	PHONE	408-240-5500
	CEO	Thomas H. Werner
	WEB	*www.sunpowercorp.com*

DESCRIPTION SunPower Corporation designs, manufactures, and markets high-performance solar electric technology worldwide. Its high-efficiency solar cells are reported to generate 50 percent more power per unit area than conventional solar technologies, and the cells' all-black appearance gives them a unique and attractive look that appeals to many customers. In 2006, the company acquired PowerLight, a leading global provider of large-scale solar power systems.

REASONS TO BE BULLISH

► The company expects to increase revenues nearly 40 percent from an estimated $700 million in 2007 to $1 billion in 2008.

► In 2008, SunPower plans to produce 250 MW and by 2009, 400 MW. It has also signed long-term polysilicon supply agreements and is ramping up its manufacturing capability in the Philippines. Both actions suggest that it will be able to achieve this growth.

► In 2007, a leading national laboratory rated SunPower's solar cell as having the highest efficiency level of any commercially installed solar cell on the market. To the extent that higher efficiency levels will translate into smaller solar cells and faster installation times, the company should be able to increase its overall sales as well as its operating margins.

► The company received an $18 million grant from the U.S. Department of Energy in 2007 to make solar cells more competitive with other forms of energy.

► In 2007 the company, together with General Electric, installed one of the largest solar farms (11 MW) in Europe. This could portend additional future deals.

► SunPower has the stated goal of reducing the cost of installing solar systems by 50 percent by 2012.

continued

► In the past year, a number of leading companies, including Applied Materials, Tiffany & Co., and Nellis Air Force Base, have selected SunPower to supply its solar cells to their largest projects.

REASONS TO BE BEARISH

► SunPower faces stiff competition from the likes of Sharp, Mitsubishi Electric, Kyocera, and Suntech, as well as the more disruptive start-ups such as HelioVolt, Nanosolar, and Miasolé.

► Its success for the foreseeable future will remain closely tied to the continuation of generous government subsidies. Any decrease to the subsidies will have an adverse impact on its stock.

► At one time, SunPower was a subsidiary of Cypress Semiconductor. The parent company still holds 98 percent of the voting power on the board. Therefore, it is possible that the board will not always act in the individual shareholders' best interest.

WHAT TO WATCH FOR   The key to SunPower's success will be its ability to continue to increase the efficiency of its solar cells and thus decrease the amount of silicon used in the production of each cell. If it can continue to do this, the company and its stock should do well.

CONCLUSION   Bullish. The solar industry is likely to experience a good deal of consolidation over the next few years. Expect SunPower to be one of the companies still standing at the end of the industry shakeout. The only thing investors need to be mindful of is the company's price-to-earnings ratio. In mid-2007, its price was high compared to its peers. An argument could be made that its extraordinary growth potential justified this high price, but even then its forward P/E ratio looked high.

Solar Companies

STP	COMPANY	Suntech Power
	SYMBOL	STP
	TRADING MARKET	NYSE
	ADDRESS	17-6 Chang Jiang South Road, New District Wuxi, 214028, China
	PHONE	86-510-85318888
	CEO	Dr. Zhengrong Shi
	WEB	*www.suntech-power.com*

DESCRIPTION   Suntech Power is engaged in the development, manufacturing, and marketing of photovoltaic cells and modules. As of 2007, it was the world's fourth largest solar cell manufacturer.

REASONS TO BE BULLISH

▶ Suntech Power has been consistently profitable since 2003, and its revenues increased by over 150 percent in both 2006 and 2007.

▶ The company's production capacity increased from 280 MW at the end of 2006 to 480 MW in 2007.

▶ Throughout 2007, the company greatly diversified its customer base by signing up major customers in Spain and the United States.

▶ The company has signed a long-term contract with MEMC Electronic Materials to supply it with silicon wafers. This means that over 70 percent of its silicon needs are guaranteed. The price security should also give the company an advantage over other competitors who may have to pay more for silicon.

▶ In 2007, Suntech announced that it had increased the efficiency of its solar cells from 15 percent to 18 percent. By 2010, it expects to increase that level to 20 percent.

▶ In mid-2007, the company announced that it would begin construction of its first thin-film manufacturing facility in China. The plant will be operational in 2008 and have a peak production capacity of 50 MW.

▶ In 2006, Suntech acquired MSK Corporation, a Japan-based solar provider. In addition to giving the company access to the Japanese market, it also positions Suntech to expand into the building integrated photovoltaic system business.

continued

REASONS TO BE BEARISH

► In return for receiving a long-term supply of silicon wafer, Suntech granted MEMC Electronic Materials a 5 percent stake in the company. It is also possible that silicon prices will drop sharply in mid-2008, thus eroding Suntech's current pricing advantage.

► The company's extraordinary growth has come at a cost. Its gross margins have fallen for the past three years, and the rapid expansion of its manufacturing capacity has resulted in an $800 million debt.

► Solar cells are basically a commodity, and increased competition from major players such as BP Solar, Kyocera, and Q-Cells could squeeze Suntech's profits.

► Solar is still not cost-competitive with other energy sources without government subsidies. If the subsidies are decreased, the entire industry will be adversely affected.

WHAT TO WATCH FOR   Investors are encouraged to watch for three things: (1) Suntech's ability to increase the efficiency of its solar cells; (2) signs that it is expanding in the U.S. market; and (3) indications that production capacity is ramping up at its thin-film plant. As long as progress is made in all three fields, Suntech will be competitive.

CONCLUSION   Bullish. Suntech has an experienced management team and a strong technical staff. It has the ability to be the world's leading solar-cell manufacturer. The fact that it is expanding its business in the United States and moving aggressively into the production of thin-film solar cells bodes well for its mid-term prospects (through 2010); and its strong presence in China will position it well for long-term growth as that country increases its demand for clean, renewable fuel.

Solar Companies

TSL	COMPANY	Trina Solar Ltd.
	SYMBOL	TSL
	TRADING MARKET	NYSE
	ADDRESS	No. 2 Xin Yuan Yi Road, Electronic Park Changzhou, 213031, China
	PHONE	86-519-85482008
	CEO	Gao Jifan
	WEB	*www.trinasolar.com*

DESCRIPTION   Trina Solar manufactures monocrystalline ingots and wafers for use in its solar-module production. Unlike many solar companies, it is vertically integrated and does everything from producing the silicon wafer to making and installing the modules.

REASONS TO BE BULLISH

► The company went public in late 2006 and in its first quarter reported a profit of $9.5 million, which was a 107 percent increase over the previous year's quarter. During the same period, its revenues jumped almost 200 percent to $42 million.

► As a China-based manufacturer, Trina Solar has lower labor and manufacturing costs than many of its competitors. It might also enjoy preferable treatment from its home government, especially as that country seeks to bolster the amount of energy produced from solar power.

► Trina has signed a long-term $120 million deal to receive polysilicon from DC Chemical.

► It has entered into a strategic partnership with Q-Cells to supply that company with silicon wafers. The wafers, in turn, will be marketed and sold as Trina Solar modules. (The arrangement helps Q-Cell by allowing it to run its manufacturing plant near full capacity, while allowing Trina to meet the growing demand of its customers.)

► In April 2007, the company brought online a production plant capable of producing 50 MW of solar cells. By the end of 2007, production is expected to increase to 150 MW.

continued

► The average efficiency level of its existing solar cells is 16.3 percent, which is fairly competitive by industry standards.

REASONS TO BE BEARISH

► Since going public in December 2006, Trina's stock has almost tripled. It is now trading at a healthy price-to-earnings ratio, and it will need to continue to grow at a very fast rate in order to continue to justify its current price.

► In the first half of 2007 the average sale price of its solar cells dropped, as did the company's operating margins. The cause of these declines was higher-than-expected silicon prices and stiff competition. Both factors are likely to continue to exert downward pressure on Trina through at least mid-2008.

WHAT TO WATCH FOR   Trina will need to ramp up the production level of its manufacturing plant to 150 MW by the end of 2007 to stay ahead of the game. If it falls short of this goal, that will be a bearish indicator. Investors are also encouraged to look for news that it is increasing the efficiency level of its cells beyond the 16 percent range.

CONCLUSION   Neutral. In the short term, Trina looks to have peaked. Higher-than-average silicon prices and intense competition will likely drive its stock lower through mid-2008. Beyond that, the company has a good chance to be one of the larger solar companies in China along with Suntech Power and JA Solar.

Conclusion

If you are a patient long-term investor, solar represents a great area to search for some buy-and-hold opportunities. Yes, opponents are right to note that solar still accounts for only a minuscule one-tenth of one percent of the world's energy, but they are foolish to think that that percentage will not grow handsomely in the years ahead.

Just consider the world of 150 years ago. America's leading source of oil came from whales, and the idea of deriving meaningful amounts of oil from the ground was dismissed as ludicrous. Of course, over a relatively short period between 1860 and 1880, the tables were reversed and it was whale oil that was soon being dismissed as an outdated relic.

Today, many so-called energy experts matter-of-factly dismiss solar's potential and argue that only coal, natural gas, oil and gas, and nuclear power can possibly meet the world's energy needs. Perhaps they are right, but, personally, I believe it is worth investing in a few solar companies on the assumption that these experts might just be the successors to yesteryear's whale oil advocates.

Chapter Six

Wind Power: The Sky Is the Limit

In 2006, the U.S. Energy Information Agency (EIA) reported that among new energy sources, wind power was the second fastest growing source in the country after natural gas. Yet to put this in some perspective, the United States installed only 2,400 MW of wind power as compared to approximately 24,000 MW of natural-gas-generated electrical power. The net effect of this imbalance is that wind power still meets less than 1 percent of the country's total energy needs.

The EIA estimates that new wind turbines will add an additional 3,000 MW of power in 2007, and still other experts in the field expect the growth rate to continue to increase between 25 to 30 percent for at least the next five years. This has led the Electric Power Research Institute to suggest that if the wind industry can continue to make technological progress in improving the efficiency of wind turbines at the same rate it has in the recent past (the average turbine is now twice as powerful as one manufactured in the year 2000), wind power could meet 5 percent of the country's electricity needs by 2011.

This extraordinary growth is not just being fueled by technological achievements; increasing concern over global climate change has focused more attention on wind power's environmental advantages. It is a zero-emission power source (meaning that it doesn't emit any greenhouse gases) and thus represents a significantly cleaner source of power than coal or natural gas. Also, because it doesn't use any fuel, it isn't sensitive to increases in the price of oil or natural gas. Furthermore, unlike nuclear power, it doesn't create any nasty, long-lasting byproducts such as radioactive waste.

The biggest factor fueling the industry's growth, however, is the simple fact that wind remains an abundant source of energy. The United States has been called the "Saudi Arabia of wind power" because of its vast wind resources, and has an almost unlimited amount of wind resources at its disposal. This is especially true if one takes into account the potential of offshore wind farms, which have been estimated to have the ability to generate 900,000 MW of power. To understand the potential of wind power in America, it is worth noting that Denmark currently generates 20 percent of its power from wind and Germany and Spain produce over 7 percent from wind. In short, from its current level of less than 1 percent, wind power can only go up.

This realization has caused an extraordinary number of European firms, which have been busy meeting demand in these European nations, to begin aggressively moving into the United States. In just the past few years, Energias de Portugal, Portugal's largest utility, acquired Horizon Wind Energy for almost $3 billion; BP bought two wind companies, Greenlight Energy and Orion Energy which have a combined capacity of 6,000 MW; Babcock & Brown acquired Superior Renewable Energy; and Iberdrola bought Scottish Power, which, as part of the deal, gained control of Oregon-based wind developer PPM Energy.

The action does not stop there. Vestas, Denmark's largest wind manufacturer, is building a huge facility in Colorado; Gamesa, Spain's wind leader, has opened a plant in Pennsylvania; Enel SpA, Italy's largest utility, is building a 150 MW wind farm in Kansas; and both Siemens and Acciona Energia have recently completed construction on turbine plants in Iowa.

U.S. companies are not standing idly by. General Electric, the country's largest supplier of wind turbines with about 50 percent of the market, continues to innovate and is presently working on constructing a new 3.6 MW turbine that can be installed on an offshore platform to create a massive wind farm; and FPL Energy (a subsidiary of the FPL Group) has completed the construction of the largest wind farm in the United States—the 735 MW Hollow Horse facility in Texas.

All of this is important for investors because the biggest winners in the wind industry are likely to be these larger companies. This is because, in spite of some smaller companies' claims, the technological differences between most large turbines (between 1 and 3.6 MW) aren't significant. Therefore, the companies that can achieve economies of scale in the manufacturing will likely be the ones best positioned to achieve the margins that allow them to remain profitable and grow the fastest.

This is not to imply that only large wind turbine manufacturers will be successful. This chapter will review a handful of the other, smaller publicly traded wind companies that are attempting to carve out successful niches in the wind power sector.

Keep an Eye on Uncle Sam

The more immediate risk to consider when investing in wind companies is that in spite of the industry's growth and dramatic improvements in technology, wind power is still not price-competitive with other sources of energy such as coal and nuclear. Therefore, investors will want to pay very close attention to the status of the tax credits the industry is receiving. Currently, wind developers receive a tax credit of 1.9 cents per kilowatt for the first ten years a wind turbine is in existence. Typically, this reduces the cost of an average $1.5 million turbine by $500,000—a discount of one-third.

The problem is that this tax credit is set to expire at the end of 2008. If it is not renewed, the industry could be thrown into turmoil much as it was in 2004 when the tax credit was temporarily allowed to lapse. During this hiatus, sales ground to a near halt.

The prospects of the wind tax credit being renewed are, however, quite favorable. Politicians are increasingly sensitive to their constituents' concerns over global climate change as well as their calls for "energy independence." Add to this the wind industry's ability to deliver new manufacturing jobs, and this combination of factors makes renewal quite likely. Still, investors should not be lulled into believing that renewal is guaranteed. Opposition from other energy providers, growing concerns over the federal budget deficit, and even unease at the prospect that the tax credit is benefiting foreign companies (Vestas, Gamesa, Siemens, etc.) as much as American companies could cause the popularity of the credit to wane.

It is also possible that growing concerns over the physical appearance of massive wind farms could cause some consumer backlash. So far there have been a few, limited instances of homeowners opposing the siting of wind farms near their property because they don't like the looks of the turbines. And still other opponents claim that the wind farms are harmful to birds, although this hasn't really been demonstrated in any meaningful way—in fact, cats and buildings both kill vastly more birds than windmills. Still, such objections could plausibly hinder the industry's growth.

These concerns, however, pale in comparison to wind's real problem, which is that it is an intermittent source of energy. That is, the wind doesn't always blow and customers need energy on a consistent and reliable basis.

To be sure, the issue is a legitimate one, but investors need to realize that in most cases wind power is not meant to entirely replace one type of energy; rather, it is meant to supplement an existing source. Furthermore, wind engineers are getting increasingly sophisticated at constructing new turbines that can generate power at lower speeds. They are also getting better at creating sophisticated wind maps that allow power companies to better estimate when the turbines will be creating power, as well as siting turbines in multiple locations so that interruptions to the overall system occur with less frequency.

Finally, the problem of wind turbines' intermittency is expected to be further minimized in the future as wind and solar power begin working in conjunction. The two energy sources complement each other well, because the conditions for solar power (i.e., sunny days) tend to be better when the wind isn't blowing and the reverse also holds true—cloudy days, when solar power production is lower, tend to be windier. It is quite possible that new advances in battery technology will also help address the intermittency issue by allowing much of the excess electricity that wind creates (say during the night when demand is low) to be effectively stored until it is needed.

Overall, though, demand for wind power is expected to remain intense. Given the high likelihood that other state legislatures will follow California, Minnesota, and Montana's lead and impose stringent renewable energy standards of between 15 and 25 percent, demand could grow even more quickly. And in the event the federal government imposes a renewable energy standard and mandates that, say, 15 percent of all electricity is to come from renewable sources by 2020, demand for wind power could skyrocket.

Regardless of such legislation, though, the prospects for the wind industry for the next five years appear bullish for the simple reason that the price of wind power in certain regions of the country is becoming competitive with other sources. It is only likely to become more competitive, bringing with it the prospect of demand continuing to outpace supply for the near future. And this means that the industry should be able to accommodate a number of wind turbine suppliers for at least the next few years.

Wind Power Companies

CWP	COMPANY	Clipper Windpower
	SYMBOL	CWP
	TRADING MARKET	London Stock Exchange's Alternative Investment Market
	ADDRESS	6305 Carpinteria Avenue, Suite 300 Carpinteria, CA 93013
	PHONE	888-702-4663
	CEO	James Dehlsen
	WEB	*www.clipperwind.com*

DESCRIPTION   Clipper Windpower is a rapidly growing wind energy technology, turbine manufacturing, and wind project development company. It has a large 215,000-square-foot manufacturing facility in Cedar Rapids, Iowa, and has wind power projects in both the United States and Europe.

REASONS TO BE BULLISH
► Clipper is well positioned for growth. Firm orders increased from 150 in 2006 to 250 in 2007, and the numbers are expected to exceed 300 for both 2008 and 2009.
► In 2006, Clipper entered into an agreement to provide FPL Energy with forty of its 2.5 MW Liberty wind turbines. It was a positive indication that the turbine is competing favorably with other turbines of the same size. More importantly, the option provides for FPL to purchase an additional 380 turbines through 2010.
► Also in 2006, Clipper signed a strategic alliance to supply BP Alternative Energy with turbines capable of producing up to 2,250 MW of wind power. As part of the deal, BP will purchase 100 MW in 2007 and 200 MW in 2008.
► As more states adopt renewable energy standards and utility companies look to purchase more wind power, Clipper is well positioned to benefit.
► Clipper invests heavily in research and development, and in 2006 and 2007 it received a number of new patents that will strengthen its intellectual property portfolio.

continued

REASONS TO BE BEARISH

► Although sales have been increasing, the company's margins narrowed in 2006 and 2007 because of higher-than-expected start-up costs and procurement inefficiencies.

► Clipper is still reliant on the federal tax credit for wind development. If the credit is not extended at the end of 2008, the company will be adversely affected.

► Both FPL and BP have the right not to exercise options beyond their initial orders.

► Clipper faces considerable competition from larger and more established companies, such as GE, Siemens, Vestas, and Gamesa.

WHAT TO WATCH FOR   If FPL exercises its option to purchase more wind turbines from Clipper through 2010, and BP also does the same after 2008, it will be a very bullish indicator. Long-term investors will also want to keep an eye on the company's ability to increase net margins as production increases.

CONCLUSION   Bullish. Clipper's relationship with FPL Energy and BP Alternative Energy are a positive indication that larger companies are confident in Clipper's technology and believe it possesses the ability to handle larger orders in the future.

	COMPANY	Enercon GmbH
	SYMBOL	N/A
	TRADING MARKET	Private company
	ADDRESS	Dreekamp 5 26605, Aurich, Germany
	PHONE	0049-49-41-927-0
	CEO	Aloys Wobben
	WEB	*www.enercon.de*

DESCRIPTION   Enercon is the third largest wind turbine manufacturer in the world and the market leader in Germany with about 40 percent of the market. (Germany, with over 20,000 MW of installed wind power, is currently the largest wind producer in the world.)

REASONS TO BE BULLISH

► One of Enercon's key innovations—and what sets it apart from other wind leaders—is that it has created a gearless, direct-drive wind turbine. The device is reported to be more efficient and quieter and requires less maintenance than other turbines.

► As of May 2007, the company had installed more than 11,000 turbines in thirty countries.

► In 2007, Enercon unveiled the E112, the most powerful wind turbine in the world. It has a span of 367 feet and can generate 4.5 MW of power—enough to power 4,000 homes.

► Although it is the leader in Germany, it still exports roughly half of its turbines.

► Enercon has a strong research and development team, and the company is likely to continue to make further modifications to its turbines.

REASONS TO BE BEARISH

► Germany currently provides very generous tax incentives to promote wind power. If the government incentives are not renewed at the end of 2008, Enercon will be adversely affected.

continued

► As a result of losing a patent lawsuit, Enercon is prohibited from selling wind turbines in the United States until 2010. Because the United States is currently installing the most wind power, this will hurt the company's growth prospects for the next few years.

► The company faces stiff competition from Vestas, Gamesa, General Electric, Siemens, and Suzlon Energy.

WHAT TO WATCH FOR   Enercon's short-term strength depends on the German government's decision to continue to subsidize the wind industry. It will therefore be important to keep a close eye on the status of the German government's decision to continue to offer tax credits and subsidies.

CONCLUSION   Enercon is a private company and not currently available to individual investors. In the event it was to go public, investors would be encouraged to consider an investment. The company's strength in Germany combined with the expectation that the U.S. market will be open to the company after 2010 makes Enercon's long-term growth prospects look appealing.

EDP	COMPANY	Energias de Portugal
	SYMBOL	EDP
	TRADING MARKET	Euronext
	ADDRESS	Praca Marques De Pombal 12 Lisbon, Portugal, 1250-162
	PHONE	351-21-001-2500
	CEO	Antonio Lus Guerra Nunes Mexia
	WEB	*www.edp.pt*

DESCRIPTION Energias de Portugal (EDP) is engaged in the generation, transmission, and distribution of electricity in Portugal and Spain. In 2007, approximately 35 percent of the energy it produced came from renewable sources, primarily hydroelectric and wind power.

REASONS TO BE BULLISH

► The company is relatively low risk. Most of its earnings come from the Portugal market, which is relatively stable, and the company typically pays out a high annual dividend.

► Energias de Portugal has experienced steady, stable growth of 9 percent for the past few years and it expects to grow through 2010.

► In the past year, EDP acquired Horizon Wind Energy for $2.9 billion. The move makes the company a leader in the U.S. wind market with a market share of 9 percent.

► With such a large portion of its electricity produced from renewable sources, EDP is well positioned to profit in a carbon-constrained environment.

REASONS TO BE BEARISH

► The company delisted from the New York Stock Exchange in 2007, but only because a meager 2 percent of the volume of its shares was coming from the United States.

► As a foreign company, its shares will be exposed to fluctuations in the euro exchange rate.

continued

► Because a large percentage of its renewable energy comes from hydroelectric power, it is possible that a prolonged drought could have an adverse impact on EDP's ability to generate electricity.

► The company is considerably smaller than many of its European counterparts and could become a target for an acquisition.

WHAT TO WATCH FOR   Investors should carefully monitor EDP's ability to digest the acquisition of Horizon Wind Energy. If it is handled smoothly, the company's move into the U.S. wind market should pay healthy dividends. Investors will also want to keep a close eye on whether Energias de Portugal spins off its renewable energy sources in an initial public offering because it could offer investors a solid cleantech investment opportunity that is free of the company's exposure to its more stable utility business.

CONCLUSION   Bullish. EDP is a low-risk company and operating in a stable and well-regulated market. Moreover, its large portfolio of renewable resources makes it an especially attractive investment in the event governments around the world impose strict limits on carbon dioxide emissions. As an added benefit, EDP offers an attractive annual dividend.

FPL	COMPANY	FPL Group
	SYMBOL	FPL
	TRADING MARKET	NYSE
	ADDRESS	700 Universe Boulevard Juno Beach, FL 33408
	PHONE	561-694-4000
	CEO	Lewis Hay
	WEB	*www.FPLGroup.com* and *www.FPLEnergy.com*

DESCRIPTION Through its various subsidiaries, FPL Group engages in the generation, transmission, distribution, and sale of electric energy. It generates approximately 34,000 megawatts of capacity, serves more than 4.4 million customers (primarily in Florida), and generated over $16 billion in revenues in 2007. This makes it one of the largest utilities in the United States. It is, however, its subsidiary, FPL Energy, that makes FPL a potential cleantech investment. FPL Energy is the largest owner of wind-power-generated electricity in the country.

REASONS TO BE BULLISH

► FPL Energy is the world's leader in wind power and has forty-nine wind facilities in fifteen states. In total, it generates over 4,000 MW of wind power. It also operates three of the five largest wind farms in America, including Horse Hollow, which, at 736 MW, is the largest wind farm in the country. In mid-2007, FPL Energy began construction of a 400 MW wind farm in Colorado, which, when it is complete, will be the second largest in the country.

► The company currently benefits from a tax credit of $19 per megawatt-hour for wind facilities, and this tax credit is likely to be extended beyond December 31, 2008.

► In addition to wind power, FPL (through its operations at the Solar Energy Generating Systems—SEGS—in California's Mojave Desert) is one of the largest generators of solar energy in the country, and in the fall of 2007 announced its intention to invest $2.4 billion to construct 300 MW of solar power. It also has smaller stakes in two nuclear power plants and a hydroelectric facility in Maine. If the federal government imposes any restrictions on carbon dioxide emissions, FPL Group will be a clear winner.

continued

REASONS TO BE BEARISH

► FPL's stock has increased over 70 percent since 2006, and it is now trading at a premium to its peers. It is unlikely to continue to generate exceptional returns in 2008 and 2009.

► As one of the largest providers of electricity in Florida, the company is vulnerable to the damage that hurricanes can inflict on the region. In 2005, it was hit by hurricanes Dennis, Katrina, Rita, and Wilma.

► FPL Energy's parent company, FPL Group, is highly regulated within the state of Florida, and it is possible that regulators will not grant the company the type of rate increases management believes necessary to sustain its current level of profitability.

WHAT TO WATCH FOR   Investors will want to keep a close eye on both the rates regulators approve for the company and the status of the federal tax credits, especially for wind and solar power. If future rate increases are lower than expected or if the federal government doesn't renew the wind or solar power tax credit, it will be a bearish indicator.

CONCLUSION   Bullish. The fact that Florida's population is growing suggests that future demand for FPL Group's electricity should remain strong, and given FPL Energy's strong position in wind and solar power, the company looks to be a solid investment. The region's demand for both of these power sources should fuel further future growth. Although it trades at a slight premium to its peers, investors looking for a relatively conservative investment in the wind industry would do well to consider FPL.

GAM.MC	COMPANY	Gamesa
	SYMBOL	GAM.MC
	TRADING MARKET	European Stock Exchange (Madrid)
	ADDRESS	Pol. Ind. Agustinos, C/A s/n E-31013 Pamplona, Spain
	PHONE	34-948-3090-10
	CEO	Guillermo Ulacia Arnaiz
	WEB	*www.gamesa.es*

DESCRIPTION   Gamesa is engaged in the manufacture, supply, and installation of products in the renewable energy sector. It comprises three separate divisions: Gamesa Eolica, which manufactures wind turbines and is the company's largest division; Gamesa Energia, which is engaged in the generation of renewable energy (primarily wind power); and Gamesa Solar, which is engaged in the manufacture and sales of solar installations, including photovoltaic applications. After General Electric, Siemens, and Vestas, it is the fourth largest manufacturer of wind turbines in the world.

REASONS TO BE BULLISH

► Net profits increased 135 percent between 2005 and 2006, and sales increased 36 percent to over $3.1 billion during the same period.

► The amount of wind power the company has installed increased to 2,400 MW—an increase of 83 percent over 2005 figures.

► Gamesa is the leading supplier of wind turbines in both Spain and China, and its presence is growing fast in the United States.

► The company's wind turbines are installed all over the world, with 65 percent located in Europe, 12 percent in the United States, 10 percent in China, and the remaining 13 percent spread out over the rest of the world.

► In 2007, the company started up seven new production facilities—four in the United States, two in Spain, and one in China—to better serve its largest markets.

continued

Gamesa continued

► In the past year, Gamesa has divested itself from nonstrategic businesses, such as aeronautics, but it does have a small presence in the solar sector. Approximately 5 percent of its business can now be attributed to solar.

► In mid-2007, Gamesa announced a €100 million plan to develop new and more powerful wind turbines.

REASONS TO BE BEARISH

► In the first quarter of 2007, nets profits decreased to €21.6 million from €25 million. Given the company's extraordinary growth, the result was unexpected and could portend some managerial or capacity problems.

► Gamesa will need to continue to demonstrate increased production capacity and improved productivity if it hopes to stay competitive with GE, Siemens, and Vestas.

► In 2006, the company experienced some manufacturing problems with its turbines. The defects don't appear to be systemic but the problem does raise concerns about the company's quality control processes.

WHAT TO WATCH FOR   As the leading supplier of wind turbines to China, Gamesa has a great chance to grow its business. To this end, investors should look for continued signs of expansion in both Asia and the United States. Interested parties will also want to keep an eye on its photovoltaic business. The area is probably even more competitive than the wind industry; if Gamesa can't be competitive in the sector, it should look to divest itself from that business and concentrate solely on wind.

CONCLUSION   Bullish. With over 10,000 MW of installed wind power, Gamesa currently possesses approximately 15 percent of the world market. Provided it can continue to increase its production, its worker productivity, and its operating margins, the company will remain a solid, long-term investment.

COMPANY	Magenn Power
INVESTORS	Private (not publicly available)
ADDRESS	18 Monet Court Ottawa, Ontario, K1T 4B6, Canada
PHONE	613-482-6558
CEO	Mac Brown
WEB	*www.magenn.com*

DESCRIPTION   Magenn Power is a company in the very early stage of development that is seeking to create a lighter-than-air tethered wind turbine that rotates about a horizontal axis in response to wind.

WHY IT IS DISRUPTIVE   If the prototype is developed as planned company officials claim the system will be able to generate power with wind speeds as low as 4 miles per hour. This would be a substantial improvement over smaller stationary turbines that need wind levels to reach at least 9 mph. A second potential advantage would be that because the system can operate at heights of up to 1,000 feet—where the wind blows both harder and with more frequency—the system should produce more energy than ground-based systems. Finally, because it is tethered, the system has great portability and can be moved in response to changing wind conditions. (This portability would also make it an ideal system for providing emergency back-up energy at disaster response sites.)

WHAT TO WATCH FOR   The company first needs to raise money, and then it needs to develop an actual prototype. Until it can do these things, Magenn offers nothing other than a promising idea.

CONCLUSION   Bearish. Individual investors should stay away from this company. To repeat, it doesn't yet have an actual working prototype, nor does it have much money. It does, however, have a slick Web site and a CEO with a poor track record (two previous businesses he ran have failed), who is actively soliciting money from individual donors. At this stage, if the company had a promising, albeit risky, technology it should have been able to receive funding from the venture capital community—but it hasn't. And that should tell investors that the company is probably too risky for them as well.

COMPANY	Southwest Windpower, Inc.
INVESTORS	Altria, NGP Energy Technology Partners, Rockport
ADDRESS	1801 West Route 66 Flagstaff, AZ 86001
PHONE	928-779-9463
CEO	Frank Greco
WEB	*www.windenergy.com*

DESCRIPTION   Southwest Windpower manufactures and sells small wind turbines, including the Skystream 3.7, Air-X, and Whisper Wind, for the home and small business market.

WHY IT IS DISRUPTIVE   The company's new sleek Skystream 3.7 is a 1.8 kW wind turbine is extremely quiet (about the equivalent sound of an air conditioner) and works in wind speeds as low as 9 mph. Moreover, it can be mounted on a pole no taller than 33 feet and needs only a half acre to be sited. The device costs between $10,000 and $13,000 and can power between 40 and 80 percent of a 2,000-square-foot home. In 2007, the company expected to sell close to 2,000 units and generate $24 million in revenue. Of the dozen or so small wind turbine companies currently in existence, Southwest has been among the most successful wind turbine companies in raising venture capital and capturing the mainstream media's attention. In the past year, *Time, Popular Science, Men's Health,* and *Playboy* have all profiled the company. The *New York Times* and *Wall Street Journal* have also run stories on its technology. The company has a growing staff and a strong distribution network.

WHAT TO WATCH FOR   Southwest Power will face competition from other companies focusing on the same niche, such as Bergey Windpower and Abundant Renewable Energy, so it will be important to keep track of developments within those companies. Beyond that, potential investors will want to monitor how successfully Southwest Power is penetrating the higher-income market of homeowners who can afford the $10,000 price and have the half acre of land to install the system. (This potential market is estimated at 13 million households.) Longer term, it is feasible

continued

that the company can develop a profitable market by selling its smaller turbines in the developing world. Before that strategy is successful, though, the price tag will have to come down. To this end, investors will want to keep a close eye on the status of state and federal tax credits because that, more than anything else, will be the key to people buying the system.

CONCLUSION Neutral. At the current time, Southwest Windpower's turbines are receiving a great deal of positive press, and initial sales will likely be brisk thanks to growing demand from higher-income individuals with a strong environmental ethos. These buyers are willing to purchase the technology more to make a personal statement than because it makes economic sense. However, to be successful in the long run Southwest will need to lower the cost of its technology to around $6,000 or $7,000. At this price, the turbines can more quickly pay back the large upfront capital investment. If the company goes public, investors are encouraged to consider an investment, but before parting with any money they are advised to review the status of the company's competitors, and confirm the continued existence of state and federal tax credits for wind power.

Wind Power Companies

SUZL.BO	COMPANY	Suzlon Energy
	SYMBOL	SUZL.BO
	TRADING MARKET	National Stock Exchange of India
	ADDRESS	5th Floor Godrej Millennium, 9 Koregaon Park Road Pune 411 011, India
	PHONE	91-20-40122000
	CEO	Andre Horbach
	WEB	*www.suzlon.com*

DESCRIPTION   Suzlon Energy is the fifth largest wind energy production company in the world and the largest in Asia. The company's services include manufacturing, operations, and maintenance services, and consultancy services.

REASONS TO BE BULLISH

► Suzlon has grown at a rate exceeding 100 percent for four consecutive years, and its share of the global wind market has increased from 6 percent in 2006 to 7.7 percent in 2007.

► It is the largest supplier of wind turbines in India (the world's fourth largest market) and controls over 50 percent of the market in that country. Suzlon will likely continue to hold this position because of the very liberal tax incentives (80 percent depreciation in the first year and a ten-year tax holiday) the government offers for all wind power purchases.

► The company's success is not limited to India. It has made significant inroads into Europe, Australia, Brazil, South Korea, and even the United States. In 2006, it opened a manufacturing facility in Minnesota.

► Suzlon operates one of the largest wind parks in Asia (Vankusawade, in India), and it is building an even larger (1,000 MW) wind park in India at Dhulia.

► Within the past year, Suzlon has introduced two new turbines—the S52 600 kW and the S82 1.5 MW models. The new models should continue to fuel the company's growth.

continued

Suzlon Energy continued

▶ Its acquisition of REpower in 2007 will position Suzlon as a leader in offshore wind turbine technology.

▶ In 2007, it signed a contract to supply a total of 400 MW of wind turbine capacity to PPM Energy of Oregon.

▶ As a vertically integrated company, Suzlon is positioned to capture profits from the complete wind power value chain.

REASONS TO BE BEARISH

▶ At the present time, Suzlon still ranks behind General Electric, Vestas, Gamesa, and Enercon in the wind industry, and it will face considerable pressure from these companies as it seeks to bolster its place in the global marketplace.

WHAT TO WATCH FOR   In 2007, Suzlon acquired REpower, a German manufacturer specializing in offshore wind turbine technology. The acquisition made strategic sense, although investors will need to monitor Suzlon's ability to successfully integrate the two companies. Investors are also encouraged to focus on Suzlon's success in penetrating the Chinese market.

CONCLUSION   Bullish. In 2007, Suzlon surpassed Siemens to become the fifth largest wind turbine manufacturer in the world and its goal is to become one of the top three players within the next few years. There is a good chance the company will succeed. As the dominant player in India, it is well positioned to consolidate its strength in that country, and its recent acquisitions in Europe (REpower of Germany and Hansen Transmissions of Belgium) will make it a formidable player on that continent. Add to this Suzlon's ability to sign large deals (PPM Energy) and build a manufacturing facility in the United States, and the company's strategic situation is both diversified and well positioned to benefit from the global increase in demand for wind power over the coming years.

VWS	COMPANY	Vestas Wind Systems A/S
	SYMBOL	VWS
	TRADING MARKET	Copenhagen Stock Exchange
	ADDRESS	Alsvej 21, 8900 Randers Denmark
	PHONE	45-97-30-0000
	CEO	Ditlev Engel
	WEB	*www.vestas.com*

DESCRIPTION   Vestas Wind Systems is engaged primarily in the development, manufacture, sale, marketing, and maintenance of wind power systems. It is the world's largest manufacturer of wind turbines and presently operates more than 31,000 wind turbines in sixty different countries on five continents.

REASONS TO BE BULLISH

► As the world's largest manufacturer of wind turbines, Vestas is well positioned to benefit from the increase in global demand for wind power.

► In 2007 alone, the company received large orders from North America, Spain, Poland, and China.

► In 2007, Vestas initiated construction of a large manufacturing facility in Colorado to better serve the U.S. market. Production is expected to begin in mid-2008. It already has production facilities in Australia, China, Denmark, England, Germany, India, Italy, Norway, Scotland, Spain, and Sweden.

► As a supplier of both large (3.0 MW) and smaller (850 kW) wind turbines, Vestas has the ability to handle mid-sized projects as well as large-scale undertakings.

► Vestas is making an active push to increase its presence in China. The country currently has 1.3 GW (1,300 MW) of installed wind power but has another 1.5 GW under construction in 2007. By 2010, the country hopes to have 8 GW of wind power. If Vestas can land even a portion of this business, it will represent a sizable increase in its overall business.

continued

REASONS TO BE BEARISH

► Vestas will face considerable pressure from GE, Siemens, and Suzlon.

► Since 2006, the company's stock has increased almost 200 percent. Investors buying now may be acquiring the stock at or near its peak.

WHAT TO WATCH FOR   The demand for wind turbines will increase in the foreseeable future. What potential investors need to watch for is whether Vestas' future growth potential and its ability to increase its future operating margins will continue to justify its inflated stock price. Vestas is still of such a modest size that it remains a possible candidate for a takeover or an acquisition.

CONCLUSION   Bullish. As the world's leading wind turbine manufacturer, Vestas is well positioned to benefit from the growing global demand for wind power. At the present time, its stock is trading at a healthy premium to its more diversified competitors (General Electric and Siemens). When its price-to-earnings ratio falls more in line with those companies, investors are encouraged to consider an investment.

Wind Power Companies

ZOLT	COMPANY	Zoltek Companies, Inc.
	SYMBOL	ZOLT
	TRADING MARKET	NASDAQ
	ADDRESS	3101 McKelvey Road St. Louis, MO 63044
	PHONE	314-291-5110
	CEO	Zsolt Rumy
	WEB	*www.zoltek.com*

DESCRIPTION Zoltek Companies engages in the development, manufacture, and marketing of carbon fibers for various applications, including wind turbines.

REASONS TO BE BULLISH

► Because Zoltek's carbon fiber composites are lighter and more durable than fiberglass, the company's growth should match—if not exceed—the growth of the wind industry. To this end, revenues in 2006 increased 53 percent from 2005 levels to $92 million, and projections suggest revenues will grow to $157 million in 2007 and then $240 million in 2008.

► In mid-2007, the company signed a large deal to provide Vestas with $300 million worth of carbon fiber over the next five years.

► In 2006, BMW began exploring the possibility of using Zoltek's carbon fiber in the construction of its next-generation automobiles. If the entire car is manufactured with carbon fiber instead of steel, the weight of the automobile could be reduced 30 to 40 percent, and the improvement in fuel efficiency could be immense.

► In addition to servicing the wind and automotive markets, Zoltek's carbon fiber also has applications in the aerospace, marine, sporting goods, and oil and gas markets.

REASONS TO BE BEARISH

► In 2005, Zoltek experienced significant problems in bringing its U.S. plant online and it is still not operating at peak levels.

► Furthermore, as the company grows it will need to raise sufficient funds for expansion. In addition to diluting existing shareholder value, this expansion could push profitability out further into the future.

continued

WHAT TO WATCH FOR   With the possibility of additional deals like the $300 million order from Vestas, investors will want to look for signs that Zoltek is planning to construct new production facilities in the near future. Another bullish indicator would be if the company opens a production facility in China to service that growing market. Lastly, investors will also want to closely monitor the project with BMW. If BMW announces that it will be using Zoltek's carbon fiber in a full line of its automobiles, it will be a very positive sign.

CONCLUSION   Bullish. Although Zoltek's stock is volatile and it is currently trading at a relatively high price-to-earnings level, the prospects for its future growth look promising. The company has no problems selling everything it manufactures and the potential for additional growth should create a nice opportunity to increase its operating margins. As long as the wind industry continues to grow at 25 percent annually, Zoltek should be able to ride the wave. The only danger is that as a smaller company it might not be able to handle such rapid growth.

Conclusion

Readers will note that the chapter contained no mention of Chinese wind turbine manufacturers. This is not because there are no such companies; rather, it is because the domestic Chinese wind industry is small and fragmented. A combination of ten different companies still meets less than 25 percent of internal demand. Vestas, Gamesa, Siemens, and GE remain the leaders in China.

Nevertheless, surging demand has awakened both the Chinese government and domestic manufacturers to the industry's immense potential. And while most companies are not competitive at this time (most are still only manufacturing older "fixed pitch, constant-speed" turbines), the Chinese government is now dedicating more money to wind power research and development.

As this funding begins to yield results, investors are encouraged to keep an eye open for the possibility of Chinese wind companies testing the public markets in the form of initial public offerings. (At the current time, Goldwind is China's largest wind turbine manufacturer.) If any Chinese companies do go public, investors are encouraged to give them serious consideration, if only because their access to low-cost labor will make their manufacturing costs one-third less than American and European companies' costs to produce comparable turbines. Such an advantage in a large country with growing demand could cause one or more Chinese wind power company stocks to experience healthy appreciation over the coming years.

"Building a hydrogen economy is costly, but so is business as usual."
—Joan Ogden, *Scientific American,* September 2006

Chapter Seven

"Alternative" Alternative Energies: Geothermal Energy, Fuel Cells, Wave Power, and Clean Coal

The previous three chapters focused on the renewable energy sources that have been attracting the most investor focus. However, biofuels, wind power, and solar power are not the only renewable energy sources. There exists a handful of other options, and this chapter will focus on four of the most prominent: geothermal energy, fuel cell technology, wave power, and clean coal.

Because each energy source is so different than the others, this chapter will be structured somewhat differently than the preceding chapters. A brief introduction will be provided for each energy source and then the companies engaged in development of related technologies will be profiled.

The Unknown Alternative Energy: Geothermal Energy

It might be somewhat surprising to many people that geothermal energy—that is, using the heat from deep below the earth's surface to generate electricity—currently produces more energy than wind and solar power combined. Therefore, it is unfair to call geothermal energy an "alternative" alternative energy. It is more like the "unknown" alternative energy. But one of the reasons it is unknown is because as of 2007 it was still producing only a scant 0.36 percent of the world's energy needs, and it was not growing at near the rates of wind, solar, and biomass energy production.

But like those other energy sources, it holds the potential to do a great deal more. In 2006, an MIT-backed panel of eighteen distinguished scientists, sponsored by the U.S. Department of Energy, released a 400-page report entitled *The Future of Geothermal Energy*. Among its key findings were that the United States could generate over 100,000 MW of electricity by 2050—or enough to power 80 million homes—if the federal government would make a serious commitment to geothermal energy research and development. The group estimated that the price tag would be $1 billion.

Unfortunately, at the present time, neither the current administration nor Congress has embraced a geothermal initiative to the degree it has for biofuels, wind, and solar. In fact, the Bush administration is seeking to terminate all federal funding for geothermal research, arguing that the geothermal industry is healthy enough for private investors to pick up the funding now.

Time will tell whether the funding is cut, but the current environment for the expansion of geothermal energy remains on tenuous grounds. In 2006, the U.S. Treasury and the Internal

Revenue Service granted the industry a 5 percent increase in its tax credit—increasing the rate from 1.9 cents per kW to 2.0 cents. The problem is that the tax credit applies only until 2008 and there is no guarantee that it will be extended. Especially because of the large up-front construction costs of geothermal facilities, such uncertainty is likely to have a chilling effect on the industry because few companies will risk investing under such circumstances.

Nevertheless, it remains possible that geothermal energy will continue to grow regardless of governmental support. There are now forty-three geothermal plants operational in the United States and another eleven (with a total capacity of 3,000 MW) under development.

The world's largest geothermal producer is Chevron; in the United States, Calpine Corporation operates the largest facility, The Geysers. Other geothermal companies include Ormat Technologies, Raser Technologies, Western GeoPower Corporation, General Electric, and Geodynamics Ltd.

The main consideration for investors contemplating an investment in geothermal energy is that in the United States the upside is immense. To date, only a minuscule 3.5 percent of the geothermal base in the country has been tapped, and most of this activity has been centered in the western states of California, Nevada, Utah, and Hawaii, where hot rocks are nearer to the surface and it is thus easier to access them. As mapping and drilling technology continue to improve, however, so will the prospects for the field's growth because it will make geothermal energy in other regions of the country more accessible and, it is believed, more economical.

The benefits of geothermal energy are extraordinary. Unlike coal and nuclear, it requires no external fuel source, and unlike wind and solar it is not an intermittent source of energy. Geothermal plants also don't emit any greenhouse gases and they work around the clock. (Geothermal systems work by pumping water into the fractures around the hot rocks and then pumping that water back out in the form of steam. The steam then drives the turbines that generate the electricity.)

The one drawback of geothermal facilities, as previously mentioned, is that they are expensive to build and operate. Many experts, however, believe that they will be competitive in terms of price with other conventional energy sources, such as coal, very soon with or without government incentives.

For this reason alone, investors are encouraged to keep a close eye on the field. And if the government decides to gets serious about research and development, or if the industry does receive some longer-term assurances about the continuation of tax credits and subsidies, geothermal energy could easily expand far beyond its current 0.36 percent of the energy market.

And while it is unlikely that the United States will ever approach the level of Iceland (which currently generates 50 percent of its electricity from geothermal energy), some experts believe that it is possible for the country to generate 10 percent of all its energy needs by 2050 from geothermal energy.

Geothermal Energy Companies

CPNLQ.PK	COMPANY	Calpine Corporation
	SYMBOL	CPNLQ.PK
	TRADING MARKET	Over-the-counter (Pink Sheets)
	ADDRESS	50 West Fernando Street San Jose, CA 95113
	PHONE	408-995-5115
	CEO	Robert P. May
	WEB	*www.calpine.com*

DESCRIPTION   Calpine Corporation is a major U.S. power company that delivers over 25,000 MW of clean electricity to customers in eighteen states. The majority of its electricity is generated from low-carbon, natural-gas-fired power plants; however, it also operates The Geysers, which is the largest geothermal facility in the United States and generates 750 MW of electricity through geothermal power. This makes Calpine the largest producer of geothermal power in the United States.

REASONS TO BE BULLISH

▶ In the event the federal government imposes restrictions on carbon dioxide emissions, Calpine is very well positioned to benefit. Of the top twenty power generators in the United States, Calpine emits the least carbon dioxide. This is because the vast majority of its power comes from clean-burning gas-fired power plants (which emit only 40 percent as much carbon dioxide as coal-fired plants), and its nineteen geothermal plants emit no carbon dioxide.

▶ In mid-2007 the company restructured much of its debt and it is now paying a much lower interest rate.

▶ Calpine has received widespread recognition from organizations such as the American Lung Association and the Sierra Club and is likely to maintain its image as one of the "greenest" power companies for the foreseeable future.

▶ Although the company is in bankruptcy proceedings, its assets make it a very attractive target for private equity investors, and such investors might be willing to pay a premium to purchase the company.

continued

Calpine Corporation continued

REASONS TO BE BEARISH

► As a result of the company's previous management team decision to purchase too many natural-gas-fired plants before it could realistically begin servicing the debt on those plants, Calpine was forced to file for bankruptcy in 2005. As a result, the company now trades as a Pink Sheet stock and makes an equity investment a very risky proposition because bankruptcy proceedings could essentially wipe out all of that value.

► In spite of the restructuring, the company was still losing money as of mid-2007.

WHAT TO WATCH FOR   Everything will hinge on the bankruptcy proceedings. It is quite possible that by 2008 Calpine will be in the hands of private investors. If it is not, investors will want to keep an eye on how it is managing its remaining debt and whether it is expanding its business in both geothermal power and natural gas.

CONCLUSION   Bullish. Once Calpine can put its bankruptcy behind it, the company should come out in a much stronger position. The fact that it will remain one of the nation's largest energy producers and the cleanest (in terms of net carbon dioxide emissions) will position it well in the likely event the federal government imposes stricter limits on carbon dioxide emissions.

Geothermal Energy Companies

ORA	COMPANY	Ormat Technologies, Inc.
	SYMBOL	ORA
	TRADING MARKET	NYSE
	ADDRESS	6225 Neil Road, Suite 300 Reno, NV 89511-1136
	PHONE	775-356-9029
	CEO	Yehudit Bronicki
	WEB	*www.ormat.com*

DESCRIPTION   Ormat Technologies and its subsidiaries are primarily engaged in the geothermal and energy-recovery business. The company designs, builds, owns, and operates geothermal plants around the world. It also sells power units, including its Ormat Energy Converters, for recovered-energy-based power generation. Ormat presently derives approximately 65 percent of its revenue from the sale of electricity and 35 percent from the sale of equipment.

REASONS TO BE BULLISH

► In the first half of 2007 revenue jumped 31 percent and the company added 24 MW of geothermal energy to its portfolio.

► In 2007, Ormat signed large deals to build geothermal power plants in New Zealand, Kenya, Indonesia, and California.

► In 2007, the company signed four additional twenty-five-year Power Purchase Agreements with Basin Electric Power Cooperative for the electricity produced by its new Ormat Recovered Energy Generation facilities. It also signed another agreement with Nevada Power for the sale of power coming from a new geothermal plant that will be built in Nevada. Both deals represent a strong vote of confidence in Ormat's technology.

► Because its geothermal facilities don't produce any greenhouse gases, Ormat will thrive in a stricter regulatory environment in the event the federal government imposes a cost on carbon dioxide and nitrogen oxide (NOx) emissions.

► By reinjecting 100 percent of the geothermal fluid back into the system, its energy recovery units conserve resources and save money.

continued

► Ormat's technology is suitable for projects as small as 250 kW. Having technology that is modular in nature gives the company the ability to incrementally expand its geothermal facilities. This not only reduces the risk for Ormat customers but provides it a way to grow with its customers.

REASONS TO BE BEARISH

► In the first quarter of 2007, the company experienced a significant loss. The cause was unexpectedly high maintenance costs at its new facilities. Future facilities could experience similar cost overruns.

► The company sports a lofty price-to-earnings ratio and will need to demonstrate extraordinary growth in order to justify such a price.

WHAT TO WATCH FOR   Ormat has indicated that its geothermal plant in San Diego will be capable of producing 250 MW of geothermal power by the end of 2008. Investors are encouraged to monitor whether this goal is met. If it is, it will be a good indication that the company can continue to meet its aggressive growth plans. Investors will also want to watch for signs that Ormat is continuing to sign contracts to build geothermal facilities around the world. Finally, the government's continued support for geothermal power in the form of research and development expenditures and tax credits will be important for Ormat's continued success for the foreseeable future.

CONCLUSION   Bullish. As both a supplier of clean energy technology and a seller of much of the electricity it produces, Ormat is well positioned to benefit from the growth of geothermal energy. Because its geothermal units are modular in nature, the company can start by manufacturing smaller facilities and then adding to those facilities as its customers' energy needs grow. Investors are encouraged to consider Ormat as a possible investment if its price-to-earnings ratio is below 50 and it is demonstrating strong growth.

Geothermal Energy Companies

RZ	COMPANY	Raser Technologies, Inc.
	SYMBOL	RZ
	TRADING MARKET	NYSE
	ADDRESS	5152 North Edgewood Drive, Suite 375 Provo, UT 84604
	PHONE	801-765-1200
	CEO	Brent Cook
	WEB	*www.rasertech.com*

DESCRIPTION Raser Technologies bills itself as a "technology licensing and development" company. It operates two segments: transportation and industrial technology, and power systems. The former is focused on improving the power density and efficiency of electric motors. The latter develops geothermal electric power-generating plants and bottom-cycling operations that generate electric power from existing power plants. The company calls this dual focus a "well to wheel" strategy—generating electricity from geothermal power (the well) and transmitting that power to vehicles (the wheel) that then utilize its motor technology.

REASONS TO BE BULLISH
▶ In 2007, Raser secured the rights to eight geothermal leases in its home state of Utah. This suggests that the company may be poised to begin executing on its strategy of becoming a leader in the production of geothermal power.
▶ In 2006, the company received a grant for $500,000 to develop an advanced electric motor for the U.S. Army.

REASONS TO BE BEARISH
▶ Raser has less than $1 million in annual revenues, and most of that money comes from a single government contract. It presently has an extraordinarily high price-to-earnings ratio of 300.
▶ The company is burning money at an unsustainable rate. Worse, most of the money is going for general administrative costs and not research and development. In 2006, the company spent $15 million on the former and only $4 million on research and development. If the company were serious about achieving long-term growth, those numbers would be reversed.

continued

Raser Technologies, Inc. continued

► Raser faces a great deal of competition in both electric motor production and geothermal power production.
► The company is currently not producing any electricity from geothermal power. Moreover, the leases it has signed are just that—leases. Until Raser actually begins building these plants (which are very expensive to build), its strategy is all talk and no action.

WHAT TO WATCH FOR   Investors should watch to see if Raser is successful in extending its contract with the U.S. Army to develop its electric motor technology. If it receives the additional funding of $4.9 million, that will be a sign that there might be some promise to its technology. Investors will also want to receive confirmation that Raser is executing on its strategy of producing geothermal plants with an annual capacity of 100 MW.

CONCLUSION   Bearish, very bearish. At the present time, Raser has less than $1 million in annual revenues but is sporting a market capitalization of over $300 million. Nothing in the company's technology or strategy (short of actually building large-scale geothermal plants capable of generating 100 MW-plus of electrical power) justifies this type of valuation. Investors can expect that because of the company's cash-burn rate it will need to raise additional money in 2008. When it does, existing shareholders' value will be further diluted. Investors interested in geothermal power are encouraged to consider Ormat Technologies as a more viable investment.

Geothermal Energy Companies

WGP.V		
	COMPANY	Western GeoPower Corporation
	SYMBOL	WGP.V
	TRADING MARKET	TSX Venture Exchange—Vancouver
	ADDRESS	409 Granville Street, Suite 400 Vancouver, Canada V6C 1T2
	PHONE	604-662-3338
	CEO	Ken MacLeod
	WEB	*www.geopower.ca*

DESCRIPTION   Western GeoPower is a renewable energy company dedicated to the development of geothermal energy projects for the delivery of clean power. The company holds a 100 percent interest in the Unit 15 Steam Field located in The Geysers geothermal field in California. It is also developing Canada's most viable geothermal field—the South Meager Geothermal Project in British Columbia.

REASONS TO BE BULLISH

▶ In 2007, the company entered into a contract to supply Pacific Gas & Electric with 25.5 MW of geothermal energy from its Geysers' geothermal field. The plant is expected to be operational in 2009.

▶ In September 2007, Western GeoPower received $18.6 million in new financing from Iceland's Geysir Green Energy.

▶ As a result of the California state legislature's decision to mandate that utilities purchase at least 20 percent of their electricity from renewable energy by 2010, Western GeoPower is well positioned to supply California power suppliers with clean energy.

▶ Once its 100 MW South Meager field project is operational in 2010, the company will be similarly suited to supply clean power to utilities in Canada.

REASONS TO BE BEARISH

▶ Western GeoPower is currently losing money and will likely continue to operate at a loss until 2011 when both its California and Canadian geothermal facilities are operating at full capacity.

continued

Western GeoPower Corporation continued

► The company only began being traded as a publicly held company in late 2006, and it did so in order to finance its project in The Geysers. Because geothermal facilities are expensive to build and operate, it is possible that the company will need to issue additional shares in the near future to raise more money. This could have the effect of diluting the value of existing shareholders' stock.

► Western GeoPower will face competition from both Calpine Corporation and Ormat in the California market.

WHAT TO WATCH FOR   The success of Western GeoPower will hinge on its ability to get both of its facilities operational as quickly as possible. If the California project is delayed past 2009 or the South Meager facility is delayed past 2010, it will be a bearish sign.

CONCLUSION   Bullish. As a smaller company, Western GeoPower is a risky investment; however, its focus on the California market makes sense because so many utilities in the state are currently clamoring for renewable energy (in order to meet the 20 percent mandate by 2010). Additionally, if the Canadian government gets serious about promoting geothermal energy, Western GeoPower will be a natural beneficiary because the 100 MW South Meager facility will be the largest geothermal plant in the country when it becomes operational.

Fuel Cells: A Marathon, Not a Sprint

More seasoned investors might be surprised to see fuel cells classified as another "alternative" alternative energy—especially since fuel cell technology has been hyped as the next big thing in energy circles since early 2000, and prognostications of the coming "hydrogen economy" have been the subject of numerous recent books and articles.

In spite of all of this attention, and predictions such as Cleantech Venture Network's estimate that the fuel cell industry will grow from $1.4 billion in 2006 to over $16 billion by 2015, fuel cells will likely remain a niche technology for at least the next decade, and such a time frame puts it beyond the purview of most investors.

Unlike some analysts who predict that fuel cell technology will *never* take off, my perspective is that it is a very promising technology, but will just take much longer to mature than many of its proponents estimate.

A useful analogy to consider is the development of hybrid automotive technology. Research into the field began more than thirty years ago, but Toyota didn't begin developing its first hybrid vehicle, the Prius, until 1993. Even then, the car itself didn't make it into full-scale production until 1997, and a decade later it still represents less than 2 percent of all the vehicles Toyota sells.

Fuel cell technology is not, however, limited to automotive applications. Fuel cells can also be used as a distributed energy source for large facilities and even as a portable power source for hand-held devices.

Regardless of the application, though, fuel cells—which generate electricity through an electrochemical conversion process—face a number of obstacles that will need to be addressed before they begin gaining widespread acceptance in the commercial marketplace.

For starters, there is the issue of storage. Storing hydrogen is a difficult issue. In its gaseous state it requires large, high-pressure cylinders, and in its liquid state it must be supercooled to temperatures of –250 Celsius. Whether the device is used to power a car, operate a backup power system for a telecommunications company, or power a laptop computer, a convenient and cost-effective material will need to be developed first.

Another serious obstacle is the lack of an infrastructure system for delivering hydrogen. The issue is less serious for those fuel cells that are being used as distributed energy sources to power hospitals' military installations, and other commercial operations, but it is a serious one for automotive applications.

To understand the problem, it is helpful to know that even if General Motors and other car manufacturers do create an efficient and cost-effective fuel cell, there are only 130 gas stations in the entire country currently capable of providing hydrogen. This compares with 170,000 stations that provide gas. Over time, many of these stations can be upgraded to supply hydrogen, but at a cost of $1 million per facility such a transition is likely to take some time. (It is possible that fuel cells could instead find a home in powering the fleet vehicles of large companies or possibly even in some niche applications such as forklifts, locomotives, or marine-based applications.)

The final issue is cost. At the present time, producing hydrogen is a relatively costly process that consists of isolating hydrogen from natural compounds—be it water, natural gas, biomass, or coal. The dream, of course, is to create a clean, low-cost method of generating electricity (say from wind or solar power) and then use that electricity to electrolyze water and separate the hydrogen atoms from the oxygen atoms. Unfortunately, such technology is not yet ready for prime time.

All of these factors suggest that the development and introduction of fuel cell technology will not be a sprint, but rather a marathon. Investors are therefore advised to begin keeping an eye on the field, with special attention being paid to how niche applications develop in the areas of backup power systems for military telecommunication facilities and hospitals, as well as industrial applications such as powering forklifts. It is probably still too soon to be investing in the field, but for future reference, here are a handful of companies worth monitoring.

Fuel Cell Companies

BLDP	COMPANY	Ballard Power Systems, Inc.
	SYMBOL	BLDP
	TRADING MARKET	NASDAQ
	ADDRESS	9000 Glenylon Parkway Burnaby, British Columbia, V5J 5J8, Canada
	PHONE	604-454-0900
	CEO	John Sheridan
	WEB	*www.ballard.com*

DESCRIPTION: Ballard develops and commercializes proton exchange membrane (PEM) fuel cells and related power generation systems for transportation and stationary applications. It operates in three segments: Power Generation, Automotive, and Materials products.

REASONS TO BE BULLISH

► Ballard's PEM-based fuel cell is considered one of the better options for use in automobiles because it offers a power density that is an order of magnitude higher than other fuel cells and it can operate on reformed hydrocarbon fuels.

► Together, Ford and Daimler own over 30 percent of the company. This suggests that if either company moves aggressively into fuel cells that Ballard could benefit significantly.

► To this end, the company has over 130 fuel-cell powered demonstration vehicles in operation.

► In 2006, the company received a $22 million follow-on order from General Hydrogen to supply 2,900 fuel-cell powered forklifts.

► The company expects revenue in 2007 to reach between $55 million and $65 million—a figure that would represent a 30 percent increase over 2006.

REASONS TO BE BEARISH

► In spite of increasing revenues from 2006 to 2007, the company has seen its revenue plummet from a high of $120 million in 2003.

continued

Ballard Power Systems, Inc. continued

► To compound matters, Ballard still expects to lose almost $50 million in 2007 and is not projecting profitability until 2011.

► With only $200 million in cash, at its present burn rate, the company will be forced to go back to the markets in 2011 to raise more money.

► Because of its heavy reliance on Ford and Daimler, if Ballard fails to meet certain milestones with regard to the improvement of its PEM fuel cells, the company could risk losing the companies' support.

► To a very large degree, the development of fuel cell technology will depend on the development of a hydrogen infrastructure. This is a very costly proposition and, to date, governments have been unwilling to make any large-scale commitments toward its development.

WHAT TO WATCH FOR: Most experts agree that the wide-scale deployment of fuel cell vehicles is at least five years away (and maybe much longer). To be successful in the short to mid-term, Ballard will need to demonstrate that it is penetrating both the market for fleet vehicles and the forklifts. Indications that it is achieving either goal should be viewed as bullish signs. Investors will also want to closely monitor the status of governmental support for fuel cell technology. If it wanes, Ballard will be adversely affected.

CONCLUSION: Bearish. Slow growth, a fast cash burn rate, and a technology that does not yet appear quite ready for the prime time make Ballard a risky proposition. Fuel cell technology will eventually catch on, but it is unlikely to happen before 2012. Investors are encouraged to revisit the company in a few years' time.

Fuel Cell Companies

FCEL		
	COMPANY	FuelCell Energy
	SYMBOL	FCEL
	TRADING MARKET	NASDAQ
	ADDRESS	3 Great Pasture Road Danbury, CT 06813
	PHONE	203-825-6000
	CEO	R. Daniel Brdar
	WEB	*www.fce.com*

DESCRIPTION   FuelCell Energy is a developer and manufacturer of fuel-cell-based power plants for the commercial, industrial, and utility markets. Its high-temperature systems can generate electricity from both natural gas and biomass fuels. The company is also developing both solid oxide fuel cell technology and next-generation carbonate fuel cell and hybrid products.

REASONS TO BE BULLISH

► FuelCell's revenues (but not its profits) are growing year to year.

► The company is a leading manufacturer of large fuel cell power plants and can scale the system to supply between 300 kW and 2.4 MW per installation. This makes FuelCell Energy a strong contender to supply large enterprises such as hospitals, hotels, and other businesses that have mission-critical energy needs.

► Unlike other fuel cells, FuelCell Energy's are scalable for both distributed generation and base load electricity applications.

► In early 2007, the company won more than $200 million from the Connecticut Clean Energy Fund to provide the state with six power projects totaling 60 MW.

► In 2007, the company received orders from California State University for a 1 MW facility, and POSCO, South Korea's leading independent energy provider, for a 2.4 MW fuel cell power plant.

► As part of the deal, POSCO also took a 7 percent equity stake in FuelCell Energy, which implies that POSCO likes its prospects for future growth.

continued

► FuelCell's CEO is a former executive with GE Power Systems and also has experience with the Department of Energy. The combination suggests that he can navigate the competitive road ahead and understands how to win government contracts.

REASONS TO BE BEARISH

► The company has consistently lost money and is not expected to be profitable for the foreseeable future.

► FuelCell's current cash-burn rate is in the neighborhood of $10 million to 20 million per quarter, which suggests it will need to return to the capital market for additional financing in the near future. If so, this could dilute current shareholder value.

► The company has a record of limited sales and will need to generate a great many more sales before it can truly be competitive.

► The company faces stiff competition from competitors such as HydroGen Corporation.

WHAT TO WATCH FOR   In order to remain competitive with other alternative energy sources, FuelCell Energy will be dependent on government incentives and subsidies for some time. Investors should monitor the status of these subsidies closely. If they dissipate, any prospects for the company's success in the next few years will also decrease. Other factors that bear watching including the company's ability to lower the cost of its fuel cells (by about 15 percent) and increase the stack-life of its cells (from three years to five years). Most importantly, however, investors will want to monitor FuelCell's ability to increase the number of multi-megawatt orders that it makes. If it can increase annual production to above 100 MW annually, that will be a bullish sign. To this end, the company has indicated that it intends to expand its manufacturing capacity in Ohio and Germany. Investors are advised to watch for action on this front.

CONCLUSION   Bearish. The deal with POSCO bears watching, but even with increasing sales in South Korea, a more competitive pricing structure, and an improvement in its stack-life technology, it is unlikely that FuelCell Energy will become profitable before 2011. Investors are encouraged to place their money elsewhere.

Fuel Cell Companies

PLUG	COMPANY	Plug Power
	SYMBOL	PLUG
	TRADING MARKET	NASDAQ
	ADDRESS	968 Albany Shaker Road Latham, NY 12110
	PHONE	518-782-7700
	CEO	Roger Saillant
	WEB	www.plugpower.com

DESCRIPTION   Plug Power principally designs, develops, and manufactures proton exchange membrane fuel cell technology for telecommunications, utility, and uninterruptible power supply applications.

REASONS TO BE BULLISH

► Plug Power is currently trading at about the cash and cash-equivalent value of its stock. (Note: Its stock price at the time of this writing was $3.60 a share and the company had $190 million cash on hand.)

► In 2006, Smart Hydrogen (a joint venture of two Russian companies) invested $217 million and took a 35 percent equity stake in the company, suggesting that it sees a market for Plug Power's technology.

► In 2007, Plug Power acquired Cellex Power, a Canadian manufacturer of proton exchange membrane fuel cell power units for electric forklift trucks. The purchase could help the company gain entry to a new market.

REASONS TO BE BEARISH

► Plug Power has never made a profit since it went public in 1999. During that time it has devoured almost $570 million and it is expected to burn another $50 million in cash in 2008.

► Sales in 2006 were significantly lower than the previous year, dropping from $13.5 million to under $8 million. For the final quarter of 2007, sales were a dismal $1 million.

► In 2006, General Electric terminated its joint venture with the company.

continued

► Its major competitor, Ballard Power Systems, has growing sales and a declining burn rate.

► There is no indication that the telecommunications industry views Plug Power's fuel cells as a practical or viable supplier of its energy needs at this time.

WHAT TO WATCH FOR   Plug Power has said that its milestones for 2007 are to install 400 GenCore systems, achieve a 50 percent reduction in GenCore's support costs, reduce manufacturing costs by 25 percent, and contain its burn rate to between $45 million and $50 million. If it can do all of these things, it might at least slow the decline in its stock. Beyond these obvious steps, however, investors should watch for the following three developments: (1) increased sales of fuel cells to the telecommunications market, (2) increased sales to the South African and Russian markets, and (3) signs that its acquisition of Cellex is paying off in the form of a higher number of sales of fuel-cell-operated forklifts. A large purchase of fuel-cell forklifts by a major retailer such as Wal-Mart would be a very positive sign.

CONCLUSION   Bearish. Although the company is presently near its all-time low ($3.60) and is selling for only slightly more than its cash value, the company's burn rate suggests that the company could be out of cash by 2011. Until its sales increase substantially, investors are advised to put their money elsewhere.

Don't Catch This Wave ... Yet

On its face, wave power—the ability to capture the energy of oceans' surface waves and convert it into usable electricity—would appear to hold great potential. After all, in addition to being an abundant and fairly reliable energy source that is close to both coastal populations and transmission systems, the technology offers the added benefit of taking up less space than wind farms while creating no visual distractions.

Unfortunately, although substantial progress is being made in the area of wave power, the field has not yet approached the stage of development where investors can safely invest in the space. (There is only one operational wave power farm in existence. It is located off the coast of Portugal and is generating only a scant 2.25 MW of power. While additional wave power parks are under development in England, Scotland, and the west coast of the United States, the industry is unlikely to be generating a sizable amount of energy anytime before 2010, if that soon.)

There are, however, two publicly traded companies currently on the market (both of which are profiled) and, by some estimates, another twenty-five development-stage wave power companies, including Verdant Power, SyncWave Energy, Bourne Energy, E.ON, Fred.Olsen Energy ASA, AWS Ocean Energy, Scot-renewables, OpenHydro, Aquamarine Power Ltd., Wavegen (a wholly owned subsidiary of Voith Siemens Hydro Power Generation), Tidal Generation Ltd., and CleanTechCom.

Investors interested in the technology are advised to wait until the technology proves that it is truly scalable. But, like fuel cell technology, before it can do that it will need to overcome a number of issues. Among the more serious issues confronting the wave power industry is the powerful and destructive nature of the world's oceans. Any successful wave power technology must demonstrate that it can, first, withstand the corrosive impact of salt water and, second, handle years of violent storms. Until concerns over the equipment's survivability and reliability can be assuaged, it is unlikely to be considered a viable alternative energy source.

Other issues that will need to be addressed include a variety of regulatory and permitting issues. For instance, while most wave power equipment is not visually obtrusive, it is expected to impact marine biology and interfere with commercial fishing interests and shipping lanes. Before large-scale wave power can be established, such issues will need to be handled to the satisfaction of government regulators, business interests, and public-interest groups.

In many ways, the field of wave power can be likened to the wind power industry of the 1980s. The technology is slowly improving and it has immense potential, but it will likely take a few years before all the bugs can be worked out. Only then will companies receive governmental approval to begin constructing the type of large-scale wave power farms necessary to generate the amount of power that will capture investors' attention.

Wave Power Companies

FVR	COMPANY	Finavera Renewables
	SYMBOL	FVR
	TRADING MARKET	Toronto Stock Exchange
	ADDRESS	1111 West Georgia Street, 24th Floor Vancouver, British Columbia, Canada, V6E 4M3
	PHONE	604-288-9051
	CEO	Jason Bak
	WEB	*www.finavera.com*

DESCRIPTION   Finavera Renewables is dedicated to the development of renewable energy resources and technologies with a special focus on wind and wave power technologies. The centerpiece of its wave power portfolio is its patented AquaBuOY wave energy converter. The company is also in the process of developing two wind power projects in Canada and Ireland.

REASONS TO BE BULLISH

- ► In 2007, the company received a preliminary permit for a proposed 100 MW wave power project off the coast of Oregon. It is also pursuing wave power projects in Canada, Portugal, and South Africa.
- ► The company began construction of its AquaBuOY 2.0 wave energy converter in June 2007.
- ► Unlike other wave power companies such as Ocean Power Technologies and Ocean Power Delivery Ltd., Finavera is more diversified as result of its dual focus on wave and wind power. Thus, if wave power does not develop as a viable source of energy, the company might still be able to prosper.
- ► To this end, a 150 MW wind project is being developed in Alberta, Canada, and another wind project with a potential capacity of 175 MW is being developed in Ireland. Moreover, the company reports that it is pursuing eighteen additional wind projects with a capacity of 1,500 MW in British Columbia.

continued

REASONS TO BE BEARISH

► As of late 2007, the company remains a development-phase company, meaning that it is not generating any revenue. Moreover, it is not expected to generate a profit until 2010 at the earliest.

► Finavera will face stiff competition from other wave power start-ups, and investors can expect to see larger companies such as General Electric and Pacific Gas & Electric move into the space.

► Regulatory issues will remain an obstacle for the industry for some time.

WHAT TO WATCH FOR All of Finavera's wave power projects are currently in the permitting stage. Investors will also want to monitor how quickly the company's AquaBuOY 2.0 system transitions from the construction stage to actual deployment. Lastly, investors should monitor whether its projects in Oregon, Portugal, and South Africa all come to fruition. If so, that will be a bullish sign. But even then investors will want to see these if projects can then become profitable.

CONCLUSION Bearish. While its diversity with wind power is a benefit, the company does not appear to have size and strength to be competitive in the field, and large-scale wave power remains too untested a technology to warrant an investment at this time. Investors are encouraged to monitor the company; if it becomes profitable by 2010 an investment might make sense, provided its profits and growth projections are in line with the price-to-earnings ratio multiples demonstrated by industry leaders.

Wave Power Companies

COMPANY	Ocean Power Delivery Ltd.
INVESTORS	Norsk Hydro Technology Ventures, Sustainable Asset Management, Carbon Trust, General Electric, Commons Capital LP, Merrill Lynch Investment Managers, and others
ADDRESS	104 Commercial Street Edinburgh EH6 6NF, Scotland, UK
PHONE	44-0-131-554-8444
CEO	Dr. Richard Yemm (Managing Director)
WEB	*www.oceanpd.com*

DESCRIPTION   Ocean Power Delivery is the developer and manufacturer of the Pelamis system—arguably the world's leading wave energy converter technology. The Pelamis is a semisubmerged structure composed of massive cylindrical sections linked by hinged joints. The wave-induced motion of these joints pumps high-pressure oil through hydraulic motors, which in turn drive electrical generators.

WHY IT IS DISRUPTIVE   In 2005, the company secured its first commercial order for a wave farm. The farm is being constructed about three miles off the coast of Portugal and will generate an estimated 2.25 MW of energy, or enough electricity to power between 1,500 and 15,000 homes. Ocean Power Delivery has also secured over $20 million from such companies as General Electric and Norsk Hydro (a leading European energy company).

WHAT TO WATCH FOR   Investors should watch for signs that the project in Portugal has not run into any unforeseen obstacles and that it is generating the 2.25 MW of promised power. Beyond that, it will be imperative that Ocean Power Delivery continues to secure additional deals. In early 2007, the government of the United Kingdom named Ocean Power Delivery as one of four wave power companies to join a $43 million wave power project off the Southwest coast of England. Ocean Power Delivery is also one of the leading recipients of a large wave power project in Scotland.

CONCLUSION   Bullish. Ocean Power Delivery is the company closest to actually commercializing a large-scale wave power farm. The fact that it has established relations with leading energy companies suggests that it will be able to line up additional financing and enter into constructive partnerships in the event the projects in Portugal, England, and Scotland prove successful and it needs to expand quickly. If the company goes public, investors are encouraged to review the prospectus and consider an investment.

Wave Power Companies

OPTT	COMPANY	Ocean Power Technologies
	SYMBOL	OPTT
	TRADING MARKET	NASDAQ
	ADDRESS	1590 Reed Road Pennington, NJ 08534
	PHONE	609-730-0400
	CEO	Dr. George W. Taylor
	WEB	*www.oceanpowertechnologies.com*

DESCRIPTION   Started in 1994, Ocean Power Technologies has developed its own proprietary PowerBuoy technology, which captures wave energy using large floating buoys anchored to the seabed. The up and down motion of the device is converted to electrical energy, and this power is then transferred via a cable to an onshore transmission system. The company has been publicly traded on the London Stock Exchange since 2003 but was listed on NASDAQ in April 2007.

REASONS TO BE BULLISH
► Ocean Power Technologies' process is currently being investigated in a number of wave power pilot projects around the world. In Southwest England, it is part of the $43 million WestWave project with three other companies, including Ocean Power Delivery and E.ON UK.
► In August of 2007, the company signed a deal with PNGC Power to fund a demonstration project in Oregon.
► In early 2007, the company received regulatory approval to proceed with the pilot project off the coast of Oregon, and its technology is also being considered for projects in Spain and South Africa
► While Ocean Power Technologies' methodology is still in the early stages of development, it is quite possible that, like wind power, wave power will continue to get better and will eventually be competitive with other forms of power.
► Because wave power utilizes less space than wind power and doesn't have the same aesthetic issues (i.e., unlike wind turbines, wave power systems are not readily visible), it could become a formidable competitor to wind power.

continued

Ocean Power Technologies continued

REASONS TO BE BEARISH

► The company is currently losing money and is likely to continue to do so until some of its pilot projects are converted into full-scale projects.

► Ocean Power Technologies faces a good deal of competition. For instance, Finavera Renewables has also received regulatory approval to proceed with a larger wave power project off the coast of Oregon, while Ocean Power Delivery has received funding from General Electric.

► Although the company has been testing and improving its technology for more than a decade, the harsh environment of the ocean—especially the corrosive effect of salt water—has proven a formidable barrier.

► In order to compete effectively in the foreseeable future, Ocean Power Technologies and the entire wave power industry will likely need to depend on government subsidies. If the subsidies aren't renewed, the impact will be significant, and detrimental to investors.

WHAT TO WATCH FOR   The key to Ocean Power Technologies' success will be to transition its pilot projects into larger operational facilities. Investors can consider it a positive sign if the company deploys enough buoys to produce over 100 megawatts of energy.

CONCLUSION   Bearish. While wave power holds great potential, investors are encouraged to think of it like wind power in the 1980s—it will take a few years for the bugs to be worked out and for the technology to become cost-competitive with other forms of alternative energy. It may also take a few years before the industry overcomes the skepticism of potential customers, such as large-scale utilities, that wave power is a reliable and affordable form of energy.

The Black Sheep: Clean Coal

Because this book is dedicated to environmentally friendly stocks, I debated whether to include profiles of any clean coal companies, since even in its "cleanest" form, coal still emits copious amounts of carbon dioxide.

To be sure, it is a legitimate concern, but I opted to provide profiles of a few companies engaged in this area for two simple reasons. First, regardless of one's personal opinion of coal, it is an unfortunate truth that coal is the cheapest form of energy currently available (assuming that environmental costs aren't taken into consideration). Second, it is also one of the most abundant. As such, coal is likely to remain a big part of the global energy picture for at least the next two decades—and maybe longer. With this in mind, a strong argument can be made that any company engaged in the development of methods or technologies to reduce the amount of harmful greenhouse gases and contaminants deserves some consideration for being environmentally friendly.

Here, then, are some of the more promising clean coal companies:

Clean Coal Companies

CST.V	COMPANY	CO2 Solution
	SYMBOL	CST.V
	TRADING MARKET	Toronto Stock Exchange
	ADDRESS	2300 Rue Jean-Perrin Quebec City, Quebec, Canada G2C 1T9
	PHONE	418-842-3456
	CEO	Jacques Raymond
	WEB	*www.co2solution.com*

DESCRIPTION   CO2 Solution is attempting to position itself as a leader in the development, production, and marketing of products and services directed at the neutralization of carbon dioxide and other greenhouse gases. To date it has focused on the development of an innovative enzyme-based technological platform that operates by biologically capturing and transforming carbon dioxide into bicarbonate, an environmentally safe product.

REASONS TO BE BULLISH

► In early 2007, the company signed a license option and technology development agreement with Babcock & Wilcox. The fact that Babcock & Wilcox is willing to pay a modest license fee ($500,000) and assume many of the expenses associated with developing a pilot project suggests that CO2 Solution's technology has some merit.

► If the U.S. government passes legislation imposing a significant cost on the release of carbon dioxide into the environment, a number of companies will likely be willing to take a closer look at CO2's technology.

► The company has a strong patent portfolio.

REASONS TO BE BEARISH

► CO2 Solution has been in existence since 1997 and has very little to show for ten years of research and development.

► The company remains in the precommercialization stage and has never made a profit.

continued

CO2 Solution continued

▶ A number of other technological solutions have been proposed for the same problem. Companies such as GreenFuel Technologies and Synthetic Genomics may ultimately develop a cheaper, more efficient, and more elegant solution to the problem of carbon dioxide emissions.

WHAT TO WATCH FOR   The pilot project with Babcock & Wilcox is the only thing investors should focus on at this time. If Babcock decides to move to full-scale production, it will be a bullish sign.

CONCLUSION   Bearish. The lack of a commercially scalable product at this time makes CO2 Solution far too risky to recommend. The fact that the company will likely need to raise additional funds from investors at some point also suggests that any investment might soon become diluted. Finally, the field of controlling carbon dioxide emissions has too many competitors, and even if CO2's technology does pan out it is hard to imagine how larger companies with deeper pockets, stronger R & D teams, and more formidable distribution networks won't quickly move into the space and squeeze out CO2 Solution.

Clean Coal Companies

COMPANY	Coaltek, Inc.
INVESTORS	Lightspeed Venture Partners, Braemar Energy Ventures, Draper Fisher Jurvetson, Warburg Pincus, Element Venture Partners, Technology Partners
ADDRESS	2189 Flintstone Drive Tucker, GA 30084
PHONE	770-934-7030
CEO	Christopher Poirer
WEB	*www.coaltek.com*

DESCRIPTION   Coaltek converts low-grade, raw coal—the most abundant type of coal—into high-grade "clean coal" at, or below, the cost of high-quality raw coal. This ability allows the company to purchase low-cost coal (typically from the western United States) and transfer it into its processing facility in Kentucky for upgrading. Coaltek then resells the processed coal to coal-burning electric utility companies at a higher price.

WHY IT IS DISRUPTIVE   Coaltek's proprietary, patent-pending technology applies highly controlled electromagnetic energy—in the form of microwaves—to reduce moisture, ash, sulfur, and mercury to create a cleaner-burning coal. By reducing moisture content, Coaltek is able to create a coal that has a higher net energy density (up to 33 percent higher). Furthermore, by being able to "dial in" the ash, sulfur, and mercury content, Coaltek is able to create a "designer coal" that can be tailored to meet the specification of the individual boilers which utilities use. Depending on the exact characteristic, the company claims to be able to reduce SO_2 and other impurities by up to 70 percent.

WHAT TO WATCH FOR   Officials at the company are on record as saying that they are able to buy cheap, dirty coal from Wyoming for about $8 a ton and sell the end product for $30 or more. If true, the economics of Coaltek's business model certainly work. At the present time, however, its facility in Kentucky is only processing 120 thousand tons of coal. Until the facility can scale up to its peak capacity of 2 million tons a year,

continued

Coaltek's process remains little more than a promising technology of limited value. Only when it can establish additional large-scale facilities will the company become a viable force in the coal marketplace.

CONCLUSION Neutral. Coaltek faces a considerable amount of competition from companies such as Evergreen Energy, as well as other cleantech companies with disruptive technologies. However, if it can begin producing at industrial-scale levels and if it finds enough customers to produce 2 million tons a year, it could have a promising future. This is because coal is quite likely to remain one of the world's predominant energy sources for at least the next ten to fifteen years (perhaps longer), and the demand for "clean coal" will only grow stronger. Any company that develops a technology to address this reality is likely to do very well in the commercial marketplace. If the company goes public, investors wanting to dedicate a portion of their portfolio to "clean coal" should consider an investment in the company.

Clean Coal Companies

EEE	COMPANY	Evergreen Energy
	SYMBOL	EEE
	TRADING MARKET	NYSE
	ADDRESS	55 Madison Street, Suite 745 Denver, CO 80206-5423
	PHONE	303-293-2992
	CEO	Kevin Rollins (Interim CEO)
	WEB	*www.evgenergy.com*

DESCRIPTION   Formerly known as KFx, Inc., Evergreen Energy uses a proprietary process to refine abundant, low-grade (sub-bituminous and lignite) coal into a more efficient solid fuel that provides energy with lower emissions.

REASONS TO BE BULLISH
► Evergreen Energy's proprietary technology can reportedly reduce the moisture content of low-grade coal from 30 percent to between 7 and 12 percent. In effect, this increases the coal's heat value from 8,000 BTU per pound to between 10,500 and 11,000 BTU per pound.
► Beginning in the fall of 2007, U.S. clean air regulations will take effect that require industrial boilers to limit toxic emissions. Because Evergreen's technology can cut mercury content by up to 70 percent, and sulfur dioxide (SO_2), nitrogen oxide (NOx), and carbon dioxide (CO_2) by measurable amounts, it should find a receptive market.
► The production of higher-grade eastern Appalachian coal, which has a higher net energy density and burns cleaner than western coal, is dwindling in supply and its price is increasing. It is currently about five times as expensive as western coal; as it becomes more costly, Evergreen's technology will become more attractive to utilities that are seeking to control costs and limit carbon emissions.
► The company's technology does not require users to undergo an extensive or expensive retrofitting.
► In 2007, Evergreen signed a deal with Sumitomo to market its technology in the Asia-Pacific region.

continued

Evergreen Energy continued

REASONS TO BE BEARISH
- ► The company is not yet profitable.
- ► Although production is reported to be increasing at its Fort Union plant, the company is only producing a modest 500 tons of coal per day.
- ► Evergreen faces competition from smaller competitors such as Coaltek as well as larger companies.

WHAT TO WATCH FOR   Investors should watch for three things: (1) that Evergreen ramps up its production at its Fort Union plant to full capacity; (2) news that existing power-generating facilities are adopting its technology; and (3) indications that the company is making headway in the Asia-Pacific market.

CONCLUSION   Neutral. As with Coaltek, which has very similar technology, the macroeconomic picture for Evergreen and its technology is very compelling—the world needs cleaner coal. Both America and China will need to rely on coal for the foreseeable future, and as the supply of cleaner-burning Appalachian coal dwindles and more stringent environmental regulations on the emission of mercury, SO_2, NO_x, and CO_2 come into effect, the demand for Evergreen's technology should increase. Even so, the company's success rests on execution, and until Evergreen proves it can actually produce cleaner coal at industrial-scale levels and make a profit doing so, investors will want to treat its stock with caution. If the company can address these issues and if there is news that it is making substantial progress in Asia—and China in particular—the outlook could turn bullish.

Clean Coal Companies

FTEK	COMPANY	Fuel Tech, Inc.
	SYMBOL	FTEK
	TRADING MARKET	NASDAQ
	ADDRESS	512 Kingsland Drive Batavia, IL 60510-2299
	PHONE	630-845-4500
	CEO	John F. Norris
	WEB	*www.ftek.com*

DESCRIPTION   Fuel Tech provides engineering solutions for the optimization of combustion systems in utility and industrial applications worldwide. It operates two separate segments, Nitrogen Oxide (NOx) Reduction Technology and Fuel Chem Technology. The former reduces NOx emissions of flue gas from boilers, incinerators, furnaces, and other combustion sources. The latter uses chemical processes to control a variety of problems in boilers, including slagging, fouling, corrosion, and the formation of sulfur trioxide and carbon dioxide. The company also employs sophisticated software to improve both technologies and processes.

REASONS TO BE BULLISH

► Fuel Tech's technology is currently employed in only 400 units worldwide, suggesting that there is great opportunity for additional growth.

► The company's NOx control technology is reportedly able to reduce emissions by 30 to 85 percent and at a fraction of the cost of competing catalytic technologies.

► In spite of coal's many problems, need for this energy source is expected to increase in the foreseeable future. Therefore, efforts to control its harmful emissions are likely to intensify.

► By some estimates, three-fourths of the coal plants in the United States don't have technology to curb NOx emissions. Fuel Tech's technology can help address this problem.

► The growth of coal power in China is expected to increase even more rapidly than in the United States, and the market for Fuel Tech's technology could spike as China attempts to limit the smog and pollution caused by NOx emissions from coal.

continued

Fuel Tech, Inc. continued

► The company has plenty of cash on hand and no debt.

REASONS TO BE BEARISH
► Since 2006, Fuel Tech's stock has nearly tripled and, at the time of publication, it was trading at a lofty price-to-earnings ratio of 102. Even with an expected growth rate of 20 percent through 2011, the company would still have a forward price-to-earnings ratio of over 40, which is a significant premium to many of its competitors (who trade in the neighborhood of 25).
► In the second quarter of 2007, both earnings and revenues of the company dropped after two contracts with Chinese coal companies were not renewed.
► While Fuel Tech's technology is cheaper than catalytic technology, the latter is far more effective. By some estimates, catalysts can reduce CO_2 emissions by 90 percent, compared to only 30 to 80 percent for Fuel Tech's technology.
► At the present time, the company only serves a fraction of the market and it faces stiff competition from Fluor Corporation and Foster Wheeler Ltd.
► Longer term, Fuel Tech will also face competition from other NOx and carbon dioxide controlling technologies such as those of Synthetic Genomics.

WHAT TO WATCH FOR   In 2006, Fuel Tech began testing its technology at two coal plants in China. In 2007, however, those tests ended and there has been no indication that other Chinese coal companies are exploring its technology. Since Fuel Tech's future growth depends in large measure on its ability to expand aggressively into this market, investors will want to see progress (in the form of contract announcements) on this front before investing.

CONCLUSION   Bearish. At the present time, Fuel Tech's future growth prospects already appear to be priced into its stock. Unless the U.S. government imposes very aggressive environmental regulations that encourage more coal companies to utilize Fuel Tech's technology or the China market opens up more than expected, investors should view this stock with caution until its price-to-earnings ratio drops back to a more reasonable level.

Clean Coal Companies

HW	COMPANY	Headwaters, Inc.
	SYMBOL	HW
	TRADING MARKET	NASDAQ
	ADDRESS	10653 South River Front Parkway, Suite 300 South Jordan, UT 84095-3529
	PHONE	801-984-9400
	CEO	Kirk A. Benson
	WEB	*www.headwaters.com*

DESCRIPTION   Headwaters develops and commercializes technologies to enhance the value of coal, gas, oil, and other natural resources. It also owns Headwaters Technology Group, Inc., a division that is developing nanocatalysts to convert coal and heavy oils into higher-yield, environmentally friendly liquid fuels.

REASONS TO BE BULLISH

► Headwaters' nanocatalyst technology is not currently priced into the stock. The technology has the potential to significantly increase the value chain of coal by reducing the amount of NO_2 that it emits and thus making it "cleaner."

► In 2007, the company started an ethanol plant with Great River Energy. Unlike most ethanol plants, it doesn't use natural gas and instead utilizes recycled heat from a nearby coal plant. This tactic should allow the ethanol plant to compete favorably with other ethanol producers.

► The company is profitable and has grown from sales of $45 million in 2001 to over $1 billion in 2007. It has also substantially lowered its debt.

► The company's fly ash, when mixed with cement, creates concrete that is four times stronger and increases its longevity by 100 percent—from twenty-five years to fifty years. As an added benefit, Headwaters concrete produces less carbon dioxide. If a cap on CO_2 is imposed, more builders might begin using this concrete.

► Although this is a longer-term prospect and not related to its alternative energy business, Headwaters is also working to develop a new nanocatalyst that could potentially upgrade heavy oil (of which Canada has a huge reserve) by making it anywhere between 10 to 20 percent lighter.

continued

REASONS TO BE BEARISH

► The company is dependent on Section 29 of the U.S. Tax Code for a substantial tax credit (it essentially makes coal dust profitable). This code is up for renewal in 2007. If it is not renewed—and it probably won't be—the company's profits could be severely impacted (in 2004, for example, the credit accounted for nearly 40 percent of Headwaters' profits).

► Nearly 45 percent of the company's revenue comes from its home construction business, and this part of its business has taken a hit due to the slowing economy and problems in the mortgage market.

WHAT TO WATCH FOR   If Headwaters' nanocatalyst proves successful in cleaning coal or upgrading heavy oil, it will be a bullish sign. Investors are encouraged to monitor whether coal or oil companies are actively testing this technology.

CONCLUSION   Bullish. Headwaters is a conservative, contrarian cleantech investment. It sports a very low price-to-earnings ratio, but its investment in ethanol and clean coal could really pay off. There is limited downside to an investment in this company.

Conclusion

All of the alternative energies highlighted in this chapter hold great potential, and it is possible that each will be successful to varying degrees. When considering an investment in any of these technologies, investors are encouraged to keep the following historical analogy in mind.

At the turn of the twentieth century it was by no means apparent that gasoline-powered automobiles would be the chosen technology. As late as 1915, one-third of all automobiles were electric, one-third were steam-powered, and one-third ran on gasoline.

For a variety of reasons including cost, convenience, government influence, and technological advancement, gasoline-powered engines won out. The same factors will undoubtedly influence how these emerging energy sources develop. For instance, fuel cell proponents are encouraged to closely monitor developments in creating membranes and catalysts which can more efficiently generate electricity; geothermal advocates are advised to monitor the status of governmental support for the field; and wave power supporters should keep a close eye on whether the system can withstand the stress of operating all day, every day in the harsh oceanic conditions. To the extent they can receive government support to address their individual technological issues, each could become more than a niche player in the world of energy.

"America is facing a crisis when it comes to electricity. But also a tremendous opportunity."

—*The Wall Street Journal,* October 16, 2006

Chapter Eight

The Cleanest Form of Energy: Energy Conservation

The easiest, cheapest, safest and, ultimately, most effective method of controlling energy costs and associated environmental issues is to prevent energy from being used in the first place. Or as one wag once said, "If you consume a lot less of the stuff, it solves a great many problems."

Luckily, throughout today's energy system, there is an extraordinary amount of "stuff" just waiting to be saved. For instance, the Federal Regulatory Commission has calculated that American utilities could reduce peak energy demand by as much as 7 percent and, in the process, save $15 billion a year just by deploying smart meter readers and sensors in homes and businesses. The devices could be read by both the consumer and the utility company, and used to control when appliances are operated. By regulating use (or by charging consumers more during high demand periods), utilities could avoid having to power up additional power plants—which often tend to be older, less efficient coal-powered facilities—in order to meet demand.

At the present time, though, only 6 percent of all American homes are installed with smart meters. Pacific Gas & Electric is in the process of installing 9.3 million such meters in California, and the eventual payoff could be huge. If the company can reduce demand by 500 MW, it would save the company the cost of needing to build one new coal-powered electrical plant.

Another piece of low-hanging fruit in today's energy system is lighting. It has been estimated that 30 percent of electrical power generated in the United States is used to power lighting—much of it generated by highly inefficient incandescent light bulbs. Wal-Mart, General Electric, and others are now actively engaged in the process of educating consumers about the extraordinary economic and environmental benefits of switching to the newer compact fluorescent light bulbs (CFLs).

It has so far been a tough sell, primarily because the bulbs are six to eight times as expensive as regular light bulbs. The upside is that the bulbs use 80 percent less electricity and last up to 12,000 hours (as compared to 1,000 hours for an average incandescent light bulb). This means that the bulbs pay for themselves in as little as six months. Over the lifetime of that bulb, the savings amount to $38 per bulb.

More significantly, if every one of America's 110 million households swapped out just one incandescent bulb for a CFL, the country would save enough electricity to power 1.5 million homes, or the equivalent of needing to build three new 500 MW coal-powered plants.

The opportunity does not stop there, however. Beyond CFL lighting, other companies, including Color Kinetics and Cree Inc., are developing light-emitting diodes (LEDs), which are even more energy efficient and whose positive impact on the environment could be more dramatic than CFLs' if the technology gains widespread consumer acceptance.

A second area ripe for saving massive amounts of energy can be found in the home and office building insulation market. Close to 80 percent of all buildings in this country were built before 1980. Since that time, remarkable progress has been made in designing and building with more energy-efficient materials; as a result of new advances in nanotechnology, next-generation insulating materials offer even more promise.

As states and local municipalities rewrite their building codes and consumers get more savvy about the savings such materials offer, the opportunity to cut down on energy consumption by using new, stronger, lighter, and better insulating materials, such as Aspen Aerogels is now making, is immense.

A related opportunity can be found in the deployment of new sensors throughout new buildings. These small, relatively low-cost devices (whose price is constantly dropping) can be used to do everything from automatically adjusting the lighting in a room when it isn't being used to providing users the ability to remotely control air conditioners and refrigerators in their homes via the Internet or possibly even their mobile phone. These capabilities are still a few years away from widespread commercial marketplace availability, but they could allow utility companies to "shave the peak" and reduce consumer energy use when demand is at its highest.

Another area offering great potential for savings lies in upgrading the existing electrical transmission grid system. It has been estimated that today's transmission system loses between 8 and 9 percent of the electricity that is produced. In this era of Six Sigma management, it is hard to imagine any industry tolerating such a high level of loss, but the problem is that replacing the old copper wires that now transmit the vast majority of the electricity across the transmission grid is an expensive proposition.

Fortunately, the existing system is now so in need of repair that the federal government and utilities are getting serious about upgrading it. To understand the magnitude of the problem, however, it helps to understand that the cost of such an upgrade has been pegged at $50 billion.

One opportunity in this area can be found in the development of new, high-efficient superconductive materials, such as what American Superconductor is manufacturing, to replace the older copper wire.

The final field that appears poised for extraordinary advances in the years ahead in the area of energy conservation is battery power. Toyota, Honda, and others have made impressive gains in hybrid automotive technology over the past few years, but so far no truly groundbreaking advances have occurred. This could be about to change. Companies such as A123 Systems, EEStor, and Altair Nanotechnologies are all developing new lithium-ion batteries that can charge faster and hold their power longer. Considering that fully one-third of all carbon dioxide emissions being emitted into the environment is attributable to automobiles—and considering that the demand for cars in the United States (which is responsible for 45 percent of all automotive emissions) as well as in such countries as China and India shows no signs of abating—the impact of better battery technology on the environment could be immense.

What follows in this chapter are profiles of a handful of cleantech companies that are trying to make money and clean the environment by helping people and businesses use new technologies to limit their use of fossil fuels.

Cleantech Companies

COMPANY	A123 Systems
SYMBOL	Private
INVESTORS	General Electric, Procter & Gamble, Motorola, QUALCOMM, Sequoia Capital
ADDRESS	Arsenal on the Charles, 321 Arsenal Street Watertown, MA 02472
PHONE	617-778-5700
CEO	David Vieau
WEB	*www.a123systems.com*

DESCRIPTION   A123 is a developer of a new generation of lithium-ion batteries for a variety of applications, including power tools, hybrid electric vehicles, home appliances, robotics, and medical devices. The company's proprietary nanoscale electrode technology is purported to give batteries a tenfold longer life, fivefold power gains, and a dramatically faster recharge time.

REASONS TO BE BULLISH
- A123 has received over $100 million in venture capital funding to date and is positioning itself as a leader in next-generation lithium-ion batteries.
- It has been successfully selling products in the commercial marketplace since early 2006 when Black & Decker began using the company's battery cells in a line of power saws.
- In 2007, General Motors began testing A123's car battery technology. A123 has also developed a Battery Range Extender Module that can be installed in the spare tire well of most hybrid vehicles.
- A123 is developing a zero-emission hybrid fuel cell bus with General Electric.
- In 2006, the company's battery technology was named by *R&D Magazine* as one of the 100 most significant new products of the year.

REASONS TO BE BEARISH
- Sony, Samsung, Panasonic, and other, smaller start-ups are also developing lithium-ion battery technology.

continued

► The price of A123's car battery technology is quite high, and unless the price drops it is unlikely to compete successfully in the commercial marketplace.

► The company's technology has not yet demonstrated that it can effectively function in extremely cold weather (–40 Fahrenheit).

► General Motors is also testing similar equipment from Johnson Controls and Saft. There is no guarantee that A123 has the superior battery technology.

WHAT TO WATCH FOR   The most bullish sign for this company will be if General Motors or some other leading automotive manufacturer announces that it intends to use the company's battery technology in its line of hybrid vehicles. The market for these vehicles in the United States is 500,000, but that number is expected to grow to almost 4 million by the end of the decade. Longer term, news that fuel cell manufacturers are utilizing A123's technology would also be a good sign.

CONCLUSION   Bullish. This company appears to have the technology, funding, and commercial partnerships to be a leading player in the battery arena. The fact that it is already generating revenues from the sale of battery cells to tool manufacturers is a positive sign. If this company goes public, investors are strongly encouraged to consider an investment. Hybrid vehicles promise to be a real growth market and, longer term, fuel cell technology should also do well. As a potential supplier to these two markets, the company could ride both waves.

Cleantech Companies

ALTI	COMPANY	Altair Nanotechnologies, Inc.
	SYMBOL	ALTI
	TRADING MARKET	NASDAQ
	ADDRESS	204 Edison Way Reno, NV 89502
	PHONE	775-858-2500
	CEO	Dr. Alan Gotcher
	WEB	*www.altairnano.com*

DESCRIPTION   Altair describes itself as a manufacturer of unique nanocrystalline materials. The company states that its proprietary nanomaterials have a variety of applications in solar cells, drug delivery, fuel cells, and advanced batteries. In the field of battery technology, it claims to have produced a nanostructured lithium titanate material that enables batteries in hybrid automobiles to operate for hundreds of miles on a single charge and that allows the battery to be recharged within ten minutes.

REASONS TO BE BULLISH
► The company has established a relationship with Phoenix Motorcars to supply its battery technology for a limited number of Phoenix's zero-emission, all-electric sports utility vehicles.
► Altair has demonstrated some success in landing modest contracts from the U.S. government, and is likely to continue to benefit from the support of its home state senator, Harry Reid, U.S. Senate majority leader.

REASONS TO BE BEARISH
► The company has never been profitable, and is burning money at a level close to $1 million a month. At this rate, Altair will need to return to investors for additional financing as early as 2008.
► New products announced by the company have often failed to materialize. For instance, in 2003, Altair announced the development of NanoCheck Algae Preventer and predicted that the product would find a niche in the pool/spa arena. No sales have yet developed. Another announcement claiming a potential relationship to produce titanium dioxide nanoparticles for a large corporate customer has also failed to materialize to date, as has a "significant" pharmaceutical deal.

continued

Altair Nanotechnologies, Inc. continued

WHAT TO WATCH FOR   Phoenix Motorcars has indicated that Pacific Gas & Electric has made a commitment to purchase 200 of its vehicles. If this deal materializes and the automobile's batteries utilize Altair's technology, it will serve as validation of the company's technology. If the deal doesn't materialize, it will be yet another example of Altair making a big promise and failing to deliver. To this end, investors should be wary of press releases touting new products that the company claims will capture large or very lucrative markets. The company's past history has not demonstrated a promising track record of managerial competence. Investors should also not be persuaded by news that the company is being awarded modest government grants. Only announcements that demonstrate it is actually receiving real revenue from commercial customers should be accorded any significance.

CONCLUSION   Bearish. In 2007, Altair's stock price fluctuated between $3 and $4 a share. Even at the low end, a market capitalization of $150 million is quite high for a company with only $4 million in revenues. Investors should treat this stock with great caution. Altair's management team seems to lack strategic focus (in the past few years it has claimed to be pursuing products in the fuel cell, drug delivery, and material sciences segments), and given the tough competition it faces from more established competitors in the battery field such as A123 and Sony, Altair appears unlikely to generate the type of revenue that would justify its current price.

AMSC	COMPANY	American Superconductor Corp.
	SYMBOL	AMSC
	TRADING MARKET	NASDAQ
	ADDRESS	Two Technology Drive Westborough, MA 01581
	PHONE	508-836-4200
	CEO	Dr. Gregory Yurek
	WEB	*www.amsuper.com*

DESCRIPTION American Superconductor manufactures and sells products using two core technologies: high temperature superconductor (HTS) wires, which are three to five times as efficient at conducting electricity as older copper wires, and power electric converters that are beneficial in connecting off-grid energy sources such as wind turbines to the electrical grid.

REASONS TO BE BULLISH
► Two macroeconomic trends are working in American Superconductor's favor. First, worldwide demand for electricity will continue to grow, and countries, companies, and customers will need efficient methods for delivering and receiving that electricity. HTS wires can help address this issue. Second, today's existing electricity grid is old and outdated. It is vulnerable to blackouts and terrorist attacks. By some estimates it will need over $50 billion in investment upgrades in the coming decade. American Superconductor's technologies could be a big part of this upgrade.
► Due to HTS's efficiency, less cable can be used. This lowers installation costs and, more significantly, minimizes environmental siting issues because fewer cables have to be placed across people's farms and fewer city sidewalks have to be torn up.
► In 2007, the company signed a deal with Consolidated Edison (the supplier of electricity to New York City) to begin deploying its superconductive power grid technology. As part of the deal, the U.S. Department of Homeland Security is expected to invest $25 million in the project.
► To this end, the Department of Homeland Security has identified HTS wires as one of a handful of "critical technologies" for their role in modernizing the existing transmission grid.

continued

► For environmental and other reasons, over 200,000 MW of power produced by natural gas has come online in the past few years. As this gas is converted to electricity, it will need to be transferred to the grid and American Superconductor's HTS wires can help in that transfer.

► There are now more than thirty wind farms around the world utilizing the company's technology.

► American Superconductor's wires also have applications in motors, and Northrop Grumman is expected to deliver the world's first 36.5 MW ship propulsion motor to the U.S. Navy in late 2007. The motor could become the motor of choice in next-generation warships.

REASONS TO BE BEARISH

► The company has yet to be profitable and is not expected to reach that stage until at least 2009.

► In 2007, the company was forced to lay off 13 percent of its workforce in order to control losses, and sales only increased 2.6 percent, while operating losses grew 6 percent, and net losses 12 percent.

► The CEO recently sold a significant number of his shares in the company.

► At its current burn rate, the company may need to raise money through a secondary offering in 2009.

WHAT TO WATCH FOR   The deal with Consolidated Edison is only in its Phase One stage. Investors need to keep a very close eye on the status of this project. If the Secure Super Grid is deployed without problems, it will be a very bullish signal and investors can expect that other utilities around the nation will begin exploring the possibility of using American Superconductor's technology.

CONCLUSION   Bullish. As stated earlier, a few big trends favor American Superconductor's continued growth: the growing demand for electricity and the need to update today's existing electrical transmission grid. Factor in the world's growing reliance on remote sources of power, such as wind and natural gas, which will need to be transmitted in the form of electricity to the grid and it is easy to see how the company is positioned for extraordinary growth. The company is one of the largest holdings in PowerShares WilderHill Clean Energy fund.

COMPANY	Aspen Aerogels
INVESTORS	Reservoir Capital Group LLC and Rockport Capital Partners
ADDRESS	30 Forbes Road Northborough, MA 01532
PHONE	508-691-1111
CEO	Don Young
WEB	*www.aerogel.com*

DESCRIPTION   Aspen Aerogels is a leader in the production of aerogel technology—nanoporous, lightweight materials that exhibit extraordinary low-thermal and acoustic conductivity.

WHY IT IS DISRUPTIVE   Aspen's aerogels, which are also referred to as "frozen smoke" because they are composed mostly of air, have two to eight times the thermal and acoustic insulation power of traditional insulators such as foam and fiberglass. Aerogels thus have the ability to deliver enormous energy savings. The material has a variety of applications in consumer, commercial, and military markets.

WHAT TO WATCH FOR   In 2006, the company began actively marketing its aerogel blankets in the oil sands region of Canada, where they are employed as insulation on oil pipes. Aspen estimates the market will be $75 million by 2011. The company is also working with NASA, the U.S. Army, DuPont, Boeing, and General Motors on a variety of aerospace, automotive, and military applications. Investors are encouraged to watch for tangible products that serve these markets. The most lucrative market is the $20 billion home insulation market.

CONCLUSION   Bullish. Aspen is believed to be profitable, and, given its early success in penetrating the oil industry, the company appears well positioned for future growth. Moreover, profits from this market should enable it to expand into the home insulation business. Aspen is currently a privately owned company, but if it does go public in 2007 or 2008, investors are encouraged to consider an investment. It is worth noting, however, that it will be competing with Cabot Corporation and 3M in the field of high-quality insulating material, so it would not be a risk-free investment.

CLRK	COMPANY	Color Kinetics, Inc.
	SYMBOL	CLRK
	TRADING MARKET	NASDAQ
	ADDRESS	10 Milk Street, Suite 1100 Boston, MA 02108
	PHONE	617-423-9999
	CEO	William Sims
	WEB	*www.colorkinetics.com*

DESCRIPTION   Color Kinetics develops, manufactures, and licenses light-emitting diode (LED) systems. It serves a number of markets, including the theater and entertainment, retail, hospitality (casinos), architectural, and high-end residential markets.

REASONS TO BE BULLISH

► Both revenues and profits increased dramatically in the first half of 2007, and the company continues to improve both its gross and operating margins.

► Color Kinetics' products have now been installed in more than 15,000 locations around the world.

► California and Canada have mandated that incandescent light bulbs be prohibited beginning in 2012, and this will likely lead to an increase in demand for LED lighting.

► In 2007, Ford Motor Company licensed the company's technology and intends to use it to develop all of its dashboard lighting systems.

► In 2006, Color Kinetics received a $1.7 million grant from the U.S. Department of Energy to develop an LED-based replacement lamp for the 60-watt incandescent light bulb.

► The company has a strong balance sheet and over $100 million in cash.

► Color Kinetics has one of the strongest intellectual property portfolios in the industry with 68 patents issued and another 170 pending. It also invests heavily in research and development.

continued

Color Kinetics, Inc. continued

REASONS TO BE BEARISH

► The stock had a nice run-up in 2007 and is now trading at a high price-to-earnings ratio. Unless it sustains its spectacular growth, the stock could drop lower in 2008.

► Color Kinetics will face considerable competition from Cree and Nexxus Lighting as well as larger companies such as Phillips and General Electric.

WHAT TO WATCH FOR   Color Kinetics is engaged in a highly publicized competition with another company to use its LED lights to illuminate the top of the Empire State Building. If it is successful, this will be a public relations bonanza for the company and will give it increased visibility on Wall Street and among individual investors. Longer term, investors will want to look for Color Kinetics' progress in lowering the costs of its products and gaining entry in the residential home market. Investors will also want to monitor the status of legislation regarding the prohibition of older incandescent lighting. If the European Union or other governments ban the lighting, LED lighting will be one of the prime beneficiaries.

CONCLUSION   Bullish. Increasing revenues and profits, healthy gross margins, and a strong intellectual property portfolio make Color Kinetics a world leader in the emerging field of LED lighting. Investors who can handle some volatility but have a long-term investment horizon are encouraged to consider a possible investment in this company.

COMV	COMPANY	Comverge, Inc.
	SYMBOL	COMV
	TRADING MARKET	NASDAQ
	ADDRESS	120 Eagle Rock Road East Hanover, NJ 07936
	PHONE	973-884-5970
	CEO	Robert Chiste
	WEB	*www.comverge.com*

DESCRIPTION   Comverge provides energy solutions that enhance grid reliability and enable electric utilities to increase available electric capacity during periods of peak demand. Utilizing wireless technology, software, and a sophisticated network of computer processors, the company can control consumers' appliances and thus reduce electricity consumption during periods of high demand. The benefit is that consumers can shave between 15 to 25 percent off their monthly electricity bills and utility companies do not need to build new power plants to meet the demand.

REASONS TO BE BULLISH

► Comverge was the first "energy management" company to go public in April of 2007 and has something of a first-mover advantage on its competitors. This fact has been rewarded by investors who have more than doubled its stock price from $18 to $38.

► Electricity demand is growing at 15 to 20 percent annually, but supply is only growing at 5 percent. To survive, businesses and homeowners will need to reduce the amount of energy they are using—Comverge's technology helps them achieve this goal.

► The company has 4.5 million devices installed and counts over 500 utility companies as clients. In total, it controls, operates, and manages 8,400 MW.

► In the past year, the company has signed sizeable deals with Pacific Gas & Electric and San Diego Gas & Electric.

► In 2007, Comverge acquired one of its leading competitors, Enerwise, in a deal totalling $76 million.

continued

Comverge, Inc. continued

REASONS TO BE BEARISH
► The company is still not profitable and may not be so for another year or so.
► It faces a great deal of competition from companies such as Honeywell, EnerNoc, and ESCO Technologies.

WHAT TO WATCH FOR   Comverge will face competition from a number of companies; investors will want to continue to see progress in the amount of megawatts it has under control.

CONCLUSION   Bullish. Ultimately, the cleanest and cheapest source of energy is the energy that a utility company doesn't have to provide. By making these "negawatts" available to utility companies and by helping customers reduce their energy bill, Comverge is well positioned to grow for the foreseeable future as both look for ways to control costs. (A "negawatt" is simply a megawatt of energy that never needs to be produced.) The company's stock could really take off if the federal government begins regulating carbon emissions.

Cleantech Companies

CREE	COMPANY	Cree Inc.
	SYMBOL	CREE
	TRADING MARKET	NASDAQ
	ADDRESS	4600 Silicon Drive Durham, NC 27703
	PHONE	919-313-5300
	CEO	Charles Swoboda
	WEB	*www.cree.com*

DESCRIPTION   Cree manufactures semiconductor materials and devices, including light-emitting diode (LED) lighting, based on silicon carbide, gallium nitride, silicon, and related compounds. At the present time, its LED products are used in electronic components (primarily as backlighting), automotive interior lighting, and color electronic displays.

REASONS TO BE BULLISH

► The governments of both Canada and California have announced that they intend to ban incandescent light bulbs by 2012 and the European Union is considering doing the same. If this happens, the demand for LED lighting could skyrocket.

► LEDs face competition from compact fluorescent light (CFL) bulbs, but to date consumer acceptance of CFL bulbs has been slow. This suggests that LED technology might be able to leapfrog CFL technology.

► Cree possesses a great deal of experience in silicon carbide and gallium nitride, and that experience should help the company improve the quality of its LED lighting and lower its cost.

► In addition to its LED line, Cree manufactures other products, including radio frequency transistors for broadband wireless applications. This not only gives the company some product diversity, it could give the company another lucrative growth market if the transistors are utilized in next-generation WiMAX technology.

► The company has $250 million cash on hand and no long-term debt.

continued

Cree Inc. continued

REASONS TO BE BEARISH

► Cree's financial results have been disappointing for the past few years; in the first half of 2007, LED revenue actually dropped from the previous year.

► Cree's LED lights are still much more expensive than CFL bulbs and might not be readily accepted by cost-conscious consumers.

► Cree faces a great deal of competition from companies such as Color Kinetics and Nexxus Lighting as well as lower-cost Asian companies.

► In mid-2007, Cree's stock saw a nice run-up driven in part by the expectation that governments will ban incandescent bulbs. Therefore, the company is now trading at a high price-to-earnings ratio, and if sales don't increase significantly in 2008, the stock could experience a sharp decline.

WHAT TO WATCH FOR   Obviously any government action on banning incandescent lighting will be a boon for Cree. Long-term investors, however, will want to look for announcements of new LED products and signs that Cree is successfully lowering the price of its products to a level where they are more attractive to average household consumers.

CONCLUSION   Neutral. Cree has great potential, as does the entire LED industry. Until the company can actually demonstrate that it can deliver profits on a consistent basis, though, investors should be wary of this stock. Investors are also encouraged to closely monitor Cree's competitors. The LED industry is driven by technological advancements, and if one of its competitors delivers a superior product (or is able to dramatically lower the price of existing LEDs), it will spell trouble for Cree.

COMPANY	EEStor, Inc.
INVESTORS	Kleiner Perkins Caufield & Byers, ZENN Motors
ADDRESS	715 Discovery Blvd. Cedar Park, Texas 78613
PHONE	512-259-5144
CEO	Richard Weir
WEB	Under construction

DESCRIPTION   EEStor is dedicated to designing, developing, and manufacturing high-energy storage devices, and the company has reportedly developed a ceramic ultracapacitor with a barium titanate dielectric that generates an enormous amount of energy. The company's stated goal is to "replace the electrochemical battery" in everything from laptop computers and low-end electric vehicles to SUVs and even utility-scale electricity storage systems.

WHY IT IS DISRUPTIVE   If the company is to be believed, its technology will be able to produce ten times as much energy as a lead-acid battery at half the cost and without using any toxic materials or chemicals. Under such a scenario, an electric car would be able to travel 500 miles on just $9 of electricity. As an added benefit, the device is said to be able to recharge in just a couple of minutes.

WHAT TO WATCH FOR   In 2006, ZENN Motor Company of Toronto made a $2.5 million investment in EEStor and it expects to receive fifteen of EEStor's Electrical Energy Storage Units for use in its electrical vehicles by the end of 2007. If the company announces additional material progress of its batteries (e.g., being able to perform at cold temperatures) or if ZENN or Kleiner Perkins decides to make follow-on investments in the company, either event could be construed as a bullish indicator.

CONCLUSION   The lack of tangible information and the company's secretive nature make its technology very hard to assess. Nevertheless, since Kleiner Perkins and ZENN Motors have both made large investments in EEStor, it suggests that there is more than just hype behind its technology. In the event the company does go public, investors looking for a high-risk, high-reward investment may want to consider the company. Be forewarned, however, that A123, Altair, Valence Technology, NEC, and Sony are all also developing competing technology.

ENOC	COMPANY	EnerNoc, Inc.
	SYMBOL	ENOC
	TRADING MARKET	NASDAQ
	ADDRESS	75 Federal Street, Suite 300 Boston, MA 02110
	PHONE	617-224-9900
	CEO	Timothy Healy
	WEB	*www.enernoc.com*

DESCRIPTION   EnerNoc provides demand response and energy management solutions to commercial and industrial customers by remotely managing electricity consumption. The company utilizes a variety of tools, including energy analytics and controls services, to manage over 525 megawatts of electric capacity.

REASONS TO BE BULLISH

► EnerNoc can reportedly reduce electricity demand by 300 MW within minutes. This type of scale and speed will attract the attention of utilities looking to better manage their power and avoid having to buy energy on the spot market at high prices.

► The company's technology can often relieve utilities from having to build a new power plant to meet growing demand (which can be an expensive proposition) or, alternatively, from having to fire up an auxiliary power plant to meet surging demand during peak periods.

► Today, utilities are having a difficult time getting siting approval for new transmission lines. EnerNoc's technology can relieve some of this pressure by reducing demand.

► In the event the federal government imposes carbon restrictions, utilities will benefit immensely from the "negawatts" EnerNoc can produce.

► EnerNoc differs from Comverge in that it focuses more on commercial businesses and less on residential consumers.

► The company's revenue is growing quite rapidly and in the past year it signed a major expansion with San Diego Gas & Electric.

continued

EnerNoc, Inc. continued

REASONS TO BE BEARISH
► Although revenue is growing, EnerNoc is not yet profitable.
► The company faces competition from larger companies such as Honeywell.

WHAT TO WATCH FOR   The market for "demand response" system is growing and, in 2007, EnerNoc established an international sales division. If the company can begin lining up new customers in foreign markets, especially China, it will be a bullish sign.

CONCLUSION   Bullish. Often, utility companies need to build expensive power plants to keep in reserve in the event that their customers need extra energy (such as on hot summer days). The problem is that these plants require an extensive amount of capital but they only operate for a few hours every year. A better solution is to reduce the demand for electricity during these periods. This is what EnerNoc's technology does, and the technology is likely to become a more important tool for every utility.

Cleantech Companies

OXN.L	COMPANY	Oxonica
	SYMBOL	OXN.L
	INVESTORS	London Stock Exchange
	ADDRESS	Unit 7, Begbroke Science and Business Park Kidlington, UK OX5 1PF
	PHONE	00-44-1865-856-728
	CEO	Dr. Kenneth Matthews
	WEB	*www.oxonica.com*

DESCRIPTION   Oxonica is a leading producer of nanomaterials for fuel catalysis. Its subsidiary, Cerulean International, distributes the company's Envirox nanocatalyst, which helps diesel fuel burn more cleanly and efficiently.

REASONS TO BE BULLISH

▶ Envirox has been successfully tested and demonstrated to improve the fuel efficiency of diesel buses by 10 percent.

▶ The nanocatalyst also helps lower the temperature at which carbon combusts and reduces emissions by allowing the engine to operate with greater efficiency. If the government imposes restrictions on carbon emissions, Oxonica's technology could be in greater demand.

▶ The company has a strong intellectual property portfolio.

▶ It also has a partnership with BASF that could lead to high-volume production.

REASONS TO BE BEARISH

▶ In 2007, the company briefly halted trading on the London Exchange because it needed to raise additional money.

▶ In 2006, Oxonica signed a high-profile deal with Petrol Ofisi, the leading oil company in Turkey, to supply Envirox across its entire distribution network. In 2007, however, Petrol Ofisi backed out of the deal for unknown reasons. Likely possibilities are that the technology was not working as promised or it wasn't delivering the expected benefits.

continued

► Oxonica faces competition from both mid-size competitors and larger corporations such as Degussa.

WHAT TO WATCH FOR   Oxonica's success is almost singularly dependent on its ability to market and sell Envirox. Any news along this line would be a positive sign.

CONCLUSION   Bearish. Until Envirox is proven to perform on a consistent basis and begins winning over larger oil companies, the company is too risky to recommend.

Conclusion

The cheapest and cleanest form of energy that any business or person can utilize is energy that isn't used in the first place. The idea is simple, yet it hasn't been fully embraced by either corporations or consumers. Slowly, this is changing as environmental concerns have raised individual and corporate awareness about the impact of their activity on the environment. Yet however noble or well intentioned these efforts may be, they haven't really translated into action. What really matters is money, and the push toward energy efficiency is largely being driven by its potential to save people money—in many cases, lots of money.

For instance, after labor costs, energy is the second largest expense for most retailers. This fact has now caused Wal-Mart to publicly state that it intends to cut energy usage in its stores by 30 percent over the coming decade. And, ultimately, it is this type of attention that will drive new businesses and entrepreneurs alike to find ways to help the Wal-Marts of the world meet their ambitious goals. The end result will likely be an explosion of new innovations over the coming years, and the prudent investor stands to profit handsomely by being alert to the companies that are delivering these energy-saving innovations.

"Green cars, homes, offices, appliances, designs, and renewable energies will be the biggest growth industry of the twenty-first century."
—Thomas Friedman, columnist for the *New York Times*

Chapter Nine

Tracking Cleantech and Building Your Own Cleantech Mutual Fund

It should go without saying that investing can be a risky business. Nevertheless, I feel compelled to offer yet another warning that investing in cleantech will likely be more volatile than investing in older, more traditional sectors. The reasons for this have been spelled out in the preceding pages but they bear repeating. For starters, every renewable energy source is competing against the larger and more established energy sources such as oil and gas, natural gas, coal, and nuclear power. In most cases, these sources are still cheaper than renewable energy sources and will likely remain so for the near-term future. Furthermore, these industries also have powerful political constituencies, and to the degree that renewable energy must continue to rely on generous government subsidies, these vested interest groups could lobby vociferously against the continuation of subsidies for clean energy.

A second concern is that different renewable energy sources will also be competing directly with one another. For example, certain homeowners may be apt to install either a solar module on their roof or a wind turbine in their backyard but, for cost considerations, may not do both. Which system they will choose will be determined by a combination of factors including up-front installation costs, the amount and reliability of the power that the system can be expected to generate, expected payback time, ease of use, and aesthetic issues. Such concerns will also affect how businesses, governments, utilities, and possibly even entire communities choose between various renewable energy options. The bottom line is that depending on the amount of technological progress made in the different fields, some alternative energy sources can be expected to be either more or less competitive than others.

There is also the issue of intra-industry competitiveness. The debates between ethanol and biodiesel, silicon solar cells and thin-film cells, or which wind turbine manufacturer can produce the largest, most efficient turbine are all legitimate concerns and have not been adequately settled yet—and won't be for some time. Again, it is worth reiterating that the development of new manufacturing methods, new technological breakthroughs, and the availability of government subsidies could tip the scale in favor of one type of renewable energy virtually overnight.

For all of these reasons, it is imperative that investors stay abreast of advances in the field. Many advances will be covered in the leading financial newspapers such as the *Wall Street Journal*, *Barron's*, and *The Economist*, but active investors are encouraged to add a few additional sources to their daily reading list.

Among some of the more informative Web sites and blogs that will keep the reader abreast of the latest activity include:

Renewable and Alternative Energy News. The site can be found at *www.michaelppowers.com/energy/current.html* and offers a solid compilation of industry news gleaned from a variety of news sources around the world. For readers looking for a quick, one-stop site for the latest news about the renewable energy sector, it does a good job of covering the major stories.

Cleantech: http://media.cleantech.com. Another excellent site on cleantech. This Web site also covers every renewable energy sector and offers extensive coverage on the smaller fields such as wave power and geothermal energy. Frequently the site will be the first to break news, and on occasion the host of the site will offer live coverage of conferences and symposia that delve in greater detail into some of the more complex and technical aspects of clean technology. The site also contains a very useful index of the individual businesses involved in cleantech and lists all of the articles that have been written in the past about individual companies.

Greentech Media: http://blogs.greentech.media.com/cleantechinvesting. Sponsored by Rob Day, a venture capitalist with @Ventures, this blog does a splendid job of keeping readers abreast of the new developments occurring among privately owned cleantech start-ups.

The Energy Blog: http://thefraserdomain.typepad.com/energy. Another very helpful site, this blog will often take much of the news that has been referenced in other sites and provide additional insights about cleantech developments. The author, James Fraser, a retired engineer with years of experience in the field, does a good job of providing useful links for investors looking for additional information.

The one thing that these news sources, Web sites, and blogs do not do is evaluate the more complex issues that are nevertheless so important when determining a company's future prospects. Here I am speaking of assessing a company's management skills, financial strength, marketing prowess, or intellectual property portfolio. (These are issues, I might add, that often elude the most seasoned and dedicated of investing experts.)

These difficulties, in combination with the previously mentioned risks (e.g., competing against traditional energy suppliers, the threats posed by new technological developments, etc.), cause a number of investors to ask the very logical question of whether there are mutual funds or exchange-traded funds covering the cleantech space.

Luckily, the answer is yes, and for investors who don't have the time or patience to research and stay abreast of the scores of publicly traded cleantech companies, investing in one of these funds is a quick and simple way to gain exposure to a diversified mix of cleantech companies. As with individual stocks, investors are reminded to do their due diligence on these funds before investing in any one. Special attention should be paid to the philosophical approach of each fund, and monitor the "screens" that they use for selecting those companies that will compose its portfolio. Often, investors may find that their interests are different from their own. For instance, some cleantech funds include nuclear companies because nuclear power emits no carbon dioxide, but other funds don't due to concerns over the creation and storage of radioactive waste. Investors are also encouraged to pay close attention to the load charges and annual expense rates that accompany each fund.

With those caveats, here then are some of the leading cleantech funds:

PowerShares WilderHill Clean Energy Portfolio. This exchange-traded fund (ETF) trades under the symbol PBW on the American Stock Exchange. It is listed first because it most closely aligns with the term cleantech as defined by this book. The fund focuses on "greener and generally renewable sources of energy and technologies that facilitate cleaner energy." It is designed to replicate the growth and appreciation of the WilderHill Clean Energy Index. As of July 2007, the fund's top ten holdings were:

Trina Solar	(3.41 percent)
Echelon Corporation	(3.29 percent)
Ormat Technologies	(3.21 percent)
American Superconductor	(3.20 percent)
Suntech Power	(3.19 percent)
Evergreen Solar	(3.16 percent)
JA Solar	(3.14 percent)
Zoltek	(3.10 percent)
Cree Inc.	(3.08 percent)
First Solar	(3.08 percent)

The advantage of this fund is that it is an ETF and thus trades more like a stock, and when it is compared with comparable mutual funds its annual expense ratio is considerably lower—about .7 percent versus an average of 1.5 percent for most mutual funds. The disadvantage of this ETF is that it is quite volatile, and since its inception it has been trailing the NASDAQ Composite Index. Another potential weakness is that—as its top ten listing demonstrates—it is currently heavily invested in solar stocks and Chinese solar stocks in particular.

Van Eck Global Alternative Energy ETF. Another exchange-traded fund, this one trades under the symbol GEX on the New York

Stock Exchange and seeks to provide targeted exposure to companies that are engaged in the alternative energy industry. Its top ten holdings as of July 2007 include:

Vestas Wind Systems	(10.97 %)
Gamesa Corp.	(7.98 %)
Renewable Energy Corp.	(6.84 %)
Q-Cells	(5.73 %)
SolarWorld	(5.33 %)
Verbund AG	(5.21 %)
Kurita Water	(4.82 %)
International Rectifier	(4.61 %)
Suntech Power	(4.32 %)
Itron	(3.61 %)

This fund was only recently launched in May 2007 so it is too early to assess its track record, but like PowerShares Wilder-Hill it has a relatively low (.65 percent) annual fee. Investors should also note that at this time it is more heavily invested in wind power (Vestas and Gamesa) than some other funds, and has more exposure to European companies than other mutual funds and ETFs. The fund also has a screen that prohibits companies that generate less than 70 percent of revenues from alternative energy from being included in the portfolio. This precludes larger and more diversified companies such as General Electric and Siemens from being included in the fund.

New Alternative Fund. A mutual fund that trades under the symbol NALFX. This fund, which was started in 1982, has the honor of being the oldest alternative energy mutual fund in existence. The fund's top ten holdings include:

Gamesa	(4.56 percent)
Vestas Wind Power	(4.41 percent)
Schneider Electric	(4.23 percent)
Q-Cells	(4.05 percent)
Abengoa SA	(3.92 percent)
Acciona SA	(3.75 percent)
Compagnie de Saint-Gobain	(3.70 percent)
Renewable Energy Corp.	(3.56 percent)
Conergy AG	(3.41 percent)
Ormat Technologies	(3.32 percent)

The advantage of this mutual fund is its lengthy track record. Over the past decade it has returned an average annual return of 9.5 percent. The disadvantage is that the fund has a 4.75 percent load and an annual expense ratio of 1.25 percent. It also has a slightly different screen for the stocks that it selects.

Guinness Atkinson Alternative Energy Fund. This mutual fund trades under the symbol GAAEX on NASDAQ and, like the other funds, has holdings in companies involved in alternative energy. Its top ten holdings include:

PNOC Energy Development Corp.	(3.32 percent)
Renewable Energy Corp.	(3.31 percent)
Q-Cells	(3.27 percent)
Suntech Power	(3.27 percent)
Ormat	(3.25 percent)
SolarWorld	(3.25 percent)
Gamesa Corp.	(3.20 percent)
Vestas Wind Systems	(3.17 percent)
Conergy	(3.14 percent)
Iberdrola	(3.14 percent)

The fund was initiated in March 2006 and has since appreciated 16 percent. In part, this is because the fund invests in smaller, high-growth companies. It also does not attempt to maintain a diversified portfolio. For instance, nearly one-third of its holding are in solar versus only 11 percent in wind. The disadvantage of this strategy is that the fund is likely to be even more volatile than the other cleantech funds.

Building Your Own Fund

If none of these funds appeals to you, the option always exists to create your own customized cleantech fund. However, because every investor has a different set of objectives for investing, and every investor has his or her own tolerance for risk, the purpose of this section is not to design a one-size-fits-all cleantech mutual fund (although a model portfolio is offered). Rather, it is to provide the average investor with a prudent method for approaching investing in this field.

To begin, almost every financial advisor urges clients to diversify their portfolios with a mix of bonds, stocks, and some cash. More cautious investors or those who have a shorter investment horizon are encouraged to carry a heavier mix of bonds. Those who are more aggressive or who have a longer time before retirement typically invest more in equities. (I will leave it to the individual reader to determine how much, if any, they wish to invest in bonds.)

The next consideration is to diversify one's stock portfolio across a variety of industrial sectors. The logic is simple. Due to the cyclical nature of many sectors, it is unwise to invest too much in any one sector in case it experiences a downswing and drags down your overall portfolio performance with it.

The same logic applies to finding an appropriate balance between U.S. and foreign stocks. Political events, fluctuations in currency valuations, and a host of other economic factors can hit any one market particularly hard, and having a well-balanced portfolio helps hedge against such factors.

Investors should also be wary of investing too high a percentage of their portfolio in cleantech stocks. Again, it is a personal decision, but prudence would dictate that an appropriate level would be around 5 to 10 percent, with the remainder split up among various other sectors including health care, financial services, materials/chemicals, and bonds. There is, of course, some room for flexibility, especially if a portion of your cleantech portfolio includes some of the larger companies—such as those mentioned in Chapter Three—which provide investors with additional exposure to different markets.

As for investing in foreign stocks, this makes sense for diversity's sake, but it also makes sense because some of the most promising cleantech companies are located in China, Denmark, Japan, and Germany.

The next consideration is to determine how to divide up one's cleantech portfolio between large companies and small and medium-sized businesses. As a general rule, large cap stocks (over $1 billion in annual revenues) typically demonstrate less volatility, whereas small and mid-cap stocks are more prone to larger deviations.

Lastly, most financial advisors encourage keeping a certain amount of cash on hand in order to meet large unexpected expenses and to hedge against unforeseen life events—like sudden unemployment. Again, it is a prudent strategy, but for our purposes, I am going to suggest investors keep a small amount of cash on hand in the event a promising cleantech company files for an IPO—something that is likely to happen a good deal over the coming years.

With all of these factors in mind, I therefore encourage clean-tech investors to determine their own mix among these various categories: foreign and U.S. stocks, large and small cap stocks, and the various cleantech sectors: biofuels, wind, solar, energy efficiency, and a catchall category labeled "miscellaneous," which captures some of those companies that represent more aggressive innovative cleantech plays or which are pursuing one of the smaller-niche clean technologies such as wave power.

The following is a suggested portfolio for a typical forty-year-old investor wishing to pursue a moderately aggressive invest-ment strategy in clean technology.

	Large	CapMid	CapSmall
Biofuels (15%)	ADM (10%)	Andersons (5%)	N/A
Solar (20%)	Suntech (10%)	Applied Materials (5%)	First Solar (5%)
Wind (20%)	GE (5%)	Vestas (10%)	Zoltek (5%)
Energy Eff. (20%)	Siemens (5%)	Amer. Super (5%)	Color Kinetics (10%)
Misc. (15%)	Gold. Sachs (5%)	Ormat (5%)	Ocean Power Tech (5%)
Cash (10%)			

As for the remaining 10 percent, I recommend keeping it in cash in the event any of the following private companies go public in the near future: Synthetic Genomics, Iogen, Imperium Renewables, Range Fuels, HelioVolt, Miasolé, Nanosolar, Konarka Technologies, Ocean Power Delivery, Aspen Aerogels, A123 Systems, or EEStor.

The odds are that some of them will return spectacular gains in the years ahead.

Conclusion

In some ways investing in the stock market is comparable to life on the African savanna. That is to say, to survive and prosper it is essential to first avoid being slaughtered. Next, one must be smart enough, fast enough, or lucky enough to be able find someone else to prey upon.

The analogy, of course, isn't perfect, but I would encourage you to keep one example from the African savanna in mind in the years ahead as you seek to navigate the bountiful, yet treacherous, fields of green investing. The metaphor pertains to how some animals survive on the savanna by working in partnership with other animals.

One of the better-known examples is the unusual affiliation among wildebeests, zebras, and ostriches. Alone, each species is vulnerable. Together, however, this triumvirate forms an impressive survival team. You see, wildebeests have very good hearing but poor eyesight and sense of smell. Zebras, on the other hand, have only modest hearing and eyesight but are endowed with a keen sense of smell. Ostriches possess excellent eyesight. By relying on the relative strengths of the other animals, the trio can often detect predators well in advance and take the necessary precautions to keep the threat at bay. Together they can survive a long time and reach their destination.

In the same way, investing is a long-term game, and reaching one's final destination—presumably a comfortable retirement—is the goal. Diversity is an integral survival technique. This is especially true with regard to cleantech investing. As the many profiles in this book testify, there is no shortage of exciting opportunities in the field.

Some investors may be inclined to stack up on one particular sector or, worse, just one or two select stocks. I would strongly advise against this. At this stage of cleantech development, it is impossible to know not only which alternative energy source will do the best or which company (or companies) within that sector will represent the best growth opportunities.

The best way to survive and prosper is to load up your cleantech portfolio with a healthy mix of solar, biofuel, and wind companies. You may even want to add a fuel cell company, a geothermal company, or a wave power company to the mix.

The bottom line is that there is no shortage of clean and abundant energy—be it in the form of sunlight striking the earth, winds blowing through the skies or tides moving the oceans, biomass growing from the fields, or heat pulsating below the earth's surface. The $64 billion question remains: which source or sources can convert that energy most efficiently? My personal opinion is that it will be a combination of these sources and that it therefore makes sense to have companies in each field in one's portfolio.

INDEX